MEMOIR

Gucci. A successful dynasty as recounted by a real Gucci
by Patrizia Gucci

All photographs published in this book come from Patrizia Gucci's private collection.
The publisher remains available for any iconographic sources not identified.

Publishing director: Jason R. Forbus
Graphic design and layout by Sara Calmosi

ISBN 978-88-3346-906-5

Published by Ali Ribelli Edizioni, Gaeta 2021©
Series – Memoir
www.aliribelli.com – redazione@aliribelli.com

Italian edition published by Mondadori Libri S.p.a., Milano

Gucci

A successful dynasty
as recounted by a real Gucci

Patrizia Gucci

AliRibelli

To my family.

Contents

Is it real Gucci?

From the beginning of time, any brand that has reached the pinnacle of fame has had to endure the impact of counterfeit products. It has had to protect and defend itself from forgeries. And just as a product can be a fake, so too can a story – especially if linked to such a highly-renowned name and brand.

When I decided to write these lines, the story of Gucci – as the dynasty that gave rise to a fashion brand with an international calibre – was once again on everyone's lips. The reason was the filming taking place in Italy (whilst the country was still in full lockdown due to the pandemic caused by Covid-19) of Ridley Scott's film, *House of Gucci*. Starring Lady Gaga, Adam Driver, Al Pacino and many others, it was obviously all over social media – proving to be a great distraction in what was still such a dramatic period in the history of our country, to be able to focus on the lights of such glamorous and must-discussed chatter, that extended from the Aosta Valley to Lake Como, from Milan to Rome.

But let us take a step back.

It was May 2003. My sister Elisabetta and I received a call from our father's brother, Uncle Roberto. He invited us to meet Giannina Facio, wife of Sir Ridley Scott, who had contacted him by telephone. Intrigued by the offer and by the fame of the well-known director, we decided to join in on the meeting at our uncle's country house, in the hills of Florence, where Giannina Facio and her assistant had come to visit. We were seated in

9

gorgeous armchairs in the garden that was in full bloom and, as we sipped tea served with traditional English biscuits, our conversation began.

Giannina Facio informed us that her husband intended to make a film about the Gucci family. Although the most significant event in the history of the dynasty, and which had long attracted media attention, was the 1995 murder of Maurizio Gucci, the film was supposed to focus on my grandfather Aldo and my father Paolo, certainly the most interesting characters in the family history. The aim of the meeting was not only to inform us about the project but also to gain our consent.

Our surprise only added to the gratification that a director as famous as Ridley Scott was interested in the history of Gucci and that he was asking for permission, basically our consent, to tell the story of the family. We were truly convinced that a marvellous film would be made and, in the wake of such enthusiasm, we all had dinner together that evening at Villa San Michele in Fiesole, all in an extremely relaxed and almost friendly atmosphere.

Shortly thereafter, we received an elegant letter from an English screenwriter, an extremely polite note reassuring us about the veracity of the narrative and the utmost respect with which all would be handled.

However, after the meeting and the letter, we heard nothing more.

Several years passed without receiving any further news about the project. Despite our requests, Giannina Facio has never provided any updates.

On occasion, we have heard of certain announcements that Ridley Scott has made to the media but nothing really ever came of it. For the sake of scruple, we even contacted the production company, which informed us that the project had been put on hold.

Then in December 2020, the media suddenly started reporting that Ridley Scott was about to make a film about the murder of Maurizio Gucci.

As more information came to light, an increasing number of details emerged, confirming that the film would not only focus on the terrible case of Maurizio's murder but would also focus – just like in the distant original project – on a good number of the most authoritative members of the family: my grandfather Aldo, my uncle Rodolfo (Maurizio's father) and my father Paolo.

I immediately sought to determine which sources were reliable in seeking out details and points of reference. I came to discover that Ridley Scott's production would be entirely based on *The House of Gucci*, a book published in 2000 by an English journalist – Sara Gay Forden – that had never been authorised by our family.

I was stunned. No-one has ever contacted me or my sister, nor any other family members, let alone have we ever heard from Giannina Facio again, in contrast to the assurances given during the meeting at my Uncle Roberto's home.

Continuing my research, I realised with the utmost distress that much of what is contained in the book by Sara Gay Forden is inaccurate and numerous falsehoods are reported.

The journalist, for example, defines my beloved Nanna Olwen as "a servant", which was absolutely not the case since, before marrying Aldo Gucci, she was the lady-in-waiting for the Queen of Romania, before travelling to Florence in the 1920s and residing at Villa Sparta in Fiesole. It was on the occasion of a visit to the Gucci store (which had opened on Via del Parione in 1923, as per the documentation filed in the Historical Archives of the Chamber of Commerce), when in the company of the queen, that Olwen met my grandfather. They later married in Wales in 1927 and never divorced.

That's not all. My great-grandfather Guccio, as the founder of the Gucci business, is defined in the book as "a poor dishwasher" when in reality, my ancestor had left for London and was employed as a lift boy at the Hotel Savoy, at that time being the only hotel in Europe with such modernism. It was certainly not a job for just anyone.

In outlining the profile of Guccio Gucci, Gay Forden's book describes him as a 'connoisseur' of leather and its processing, when he had actually entrusted skilled craftsmen capable of transforming his brilliant ideas and intuitions into products intended to become items of excellence.

According to what Gay Forden wrote, "Cuoio grasso soon became a Gucci trademark". Yet also this is not true. My grandfather went to Scotland with my father to see the most qualified leather supplier. Together, they selected a specific quality of leather, making it an indispensable material in the production of bags and suitcases, also due to its distinctive and unique fragrance. It was then that the famous brindle was also created, which later went on to become an essential feature in Gucci productions.

Furthermore, according to that written in the book, Guccio is said to have made his children promise that control of the company would never end up in the hands of a woman. This is yet another falsehood, given that Grimalda – the eldest child and only daughter – was employed by the company for many years, leaving only once she had reached retirement age to go off and enjoy a more peaceful life.

The English writer then tells of never-ending quarrels between my grandfather Aldo and my father Paolo and talks of great offenses being committed against him with Aldo supposedly even calling Paolo an "idiota". In reality, they both had the same strong and dominant character, thus there was – quite understandably – no lack of disagreements between them. Still, Aldo never questioned the genius creativity of his son – to the contrary, he recognised and appreciated it.

One truly serious inaccuracy attributes a "second marriage" to my father, who only ever married my mother, Yvonne. The woman who is passed off as his second wife was only and solely a friend. Finally, the English journalist writes that, "Paolo left Florence for New York in 1978 and was ousted from any operational role in the company by 1982".

Again, this is untrue. Paolo actually opened his own atelier in 1978 to create Gucci products, with the aim of demonstrating to the other members of the family that he was the real creative mind in the family. He had designed a beautiful scarf inspired by Pompeii under the Gucci brand yet created by his designer Roberto Meciani. This scarf was then sent to New York to be part of an exhibition on Guccio Gucci. This move was judged as a blatant act of rivalry but that was not the case. The situation dragged on for some time, with Rodolfo continuing to complain until my exasperated father put an end to it by creating his own brand.

In 1988, my father won a lawsuit he had filed in the US against Maurizio, demonstrating that he was the only true designer of the company.

At that point, he was able to his creations: "Paolo, designed by Paolo Gucci".

I'll stop here, with just one brief and final thing to consider.

In today's world, where information travels at an impressive speed, bouncing from the media to social media and vice versa, it is not always easy to go back to the primary source and verify the details. Like weeds, fake news is difficult to eradicate.

This is all the more reason why, when approaching a story – particularly if it belongs to the family and involves many people and their most intimate and personal experiences – attention, research, measure, respect and a love for the truth are all required.

Especially if you want to make a show out of it.

Family Tree

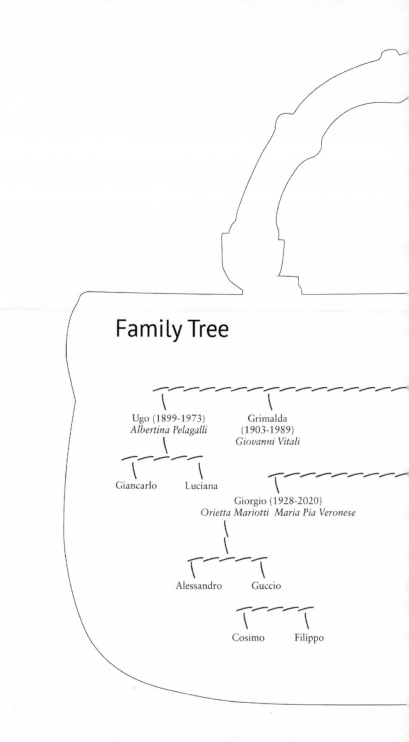

Ugo (1899-1973)
Albertina Pelagalli

Grimalda
(1903-1989)
Giovanni Vitali

Giancarlo   Luciana

Giorgio (1928-2020)
Orietta Mariotti Maria Pia Veronese

Alessandro   Guccio

Cosimo   Filippo

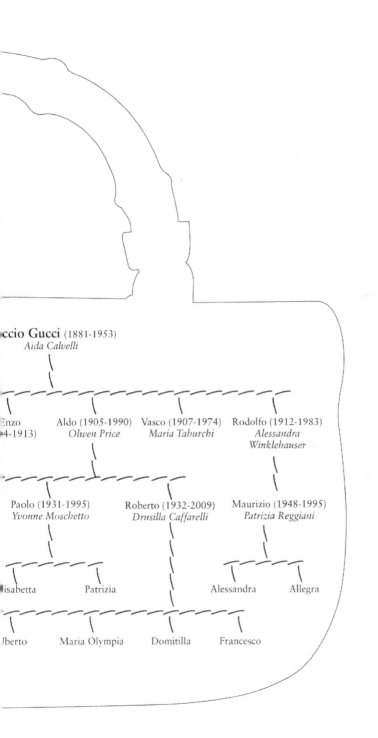

ccio Gucci (1881-1953)
Aida Calvelli

Enzo
(4-1913)

Aldo (1905-1990)
Olwen Price

Vasco (1907-1974)
Maria Taburchi

Rodolfo (1912-1983)
Alessandra Winklehauser

Paolo (1931-1995)
Yvonne Moschetto

Roberto (1932-2009)
Drusilla Caffarelli

Maurizio (1948-1995)
Patrizia Reggiani

isabetta

Patrizia

Alessandra

Allegra

Jberto

Maria Olympia

Domitilla

Francesco

Foreword

My name is Patrizia Gucci. The company bearing my surname was created in Florence by my great grandfather, Guccio, at the beginning of 1900s when it was just a small workshop.

Today, the company is a multinational but that Gucci has nothing to do with us. The last time I entered a Gucci shop, nobody even recognised me and a wound in my heart opened once again.

This is why I want to tell my story, to bear witness to the history of my family.

But let me start first of all with another loss.

My father Paolo

The memory of my father waving goodbye to me at London Airport is still engraved in my mind.

It was autumn 1995. After my father's last visit to our home in Florence, I was returning after having accompanied him back to England, where he lived. I watched his hand move as if he wanted to brush away the life that was slipping away from him – the life he would no longer live. For he died two weeks later.

How many times have I recalled that gesture that pains me so deeply to this day? It was the beginning and perhaps the end of a very long chain of events and inner searching, evidence of an intense relationship between a father and his daughter.

A few days earlier, my father had come to Florence from Sussex, where he was living with a new female companion. He had come to see my mother, Yvonne, just three months after his last visit. Though separated, they often met up and called each other. During the last telephone call, my mother had detected a strange tone in his voice. I, too, was shocked when I first saw him – he had lost a lot of weight and was quite pale.

My mother immediately gathered a team of doctors and made appointments for tests at the hospital. That night, Paolo slept alongside her and, holding her hand, confessed that she was the only woman he had ever really loved. The diagnosis given by the doctors was alarming: Hepatitis C, last stage. The only cure was a transplant that would have to be done in England, at

King's Hospital, the best in the field. However, the danger was that he might suffer kidney failure after surgery.

My father did not appear particularly alarmed when he heard the news. He had been suffering from liver problems for some time, even though he played them down. The day before leaving for England, he left some shirts to be laundered with my mother, saying he would collect them on his next visit. He hugged me tightly, as he had never done before, and even complimented me, saying how elegant I was – also something that had never happened before. It was most unusual behaviour for him.

The following day, he and I drove to the Florence airport. We were flying together to London then I would fly straight back to Italy. I helped him pack his suitcase then we tended to the waxbills, tropical red and orange birds that he was temporarily keeping in my mother's garden. My father had always had a great passion for animals and, true to his grand ways, he had just bought fifty of these passerines. He wanted to take the whole lot back with him to England but I managed to convince him to take only two, which we placed in a shoebox with holes in the lid.

Sensing he was truly unwell, I could barely hold back my tears. Yet, nothing seemed to suggest that deep inside he knew his time was drawing near. It was clear to me that he had accepted his fate. I later came to know that his doctors had given him a device that he was to have on him at all times, as it which alert him with a beep when an organ became available for a transplant. Yet, he cast the device aside, not wanting the operation out of fear that he would have to spend the rest of his life as an invalid.

Faced with losing him, I realised how much I loved him but also how much he had caused me to suffer. Although we had always had a complicated relationship, I felt I wanted to help him and ease his suffering now that we were spending our last moments together. But I didn't know how.

We left my mother's house on the hill of Poggio Imperiale, where my parents had lived together so many years and which now brought back a wave of memories.

Built in the 1960s, the house had been painstakingly designed, with large fireplaces and English-style windows looking out onto the garden. The top floor consisted of an attic and a large terrace, where my sister and I had spent much of our time – so much so that it had gradually become our special realm. It had a park that had been designed by a famous Florentine landscapist, who had a knack for making the most sophisticated garden look natural. There were sycamores, Tuscan pines, red hibiscus and iris of all colours, including the very rare black variety.

Our journey to London was not easy. We needed a wheelchair to take my father up to the plane. I walked beside him carrying his grey raincoat over my left arm, holding the shoebox with the birds in my right, making sure it would not be spotted. I made light conversation with my father but kept a watchful eye on the customs officials, fearing they would notice my compromising baggage.

In those moments, I mentally pictured the entire course of our life together: the pleasant times and the disappointments, the reprimands and the praise. It hurt me deeply to see him so tired and resigned to his fate.

For many years, since the early 1980s, my father had chosen to live in his beloved England, where he devoted himself to breeding the horses he most adored – Arabians. In Rusper, Sussex, he searched for and found a large estate with a manor house that he restored with style and elegance. On the property, he built a magnificent stable for his horses. Music was always played in the stable, as he was convinced that it cheered up the animals. Each horse had its own blanket with its name and "Stable PG" embroidered on it. The saddles too were original creations, with the dominant colours always being red and black.

Although he was now living in England, my father often came to Florence for business and also to get back in touch with his Italian side, which deep down he missed. He longed for Tuscan food and so off we would go to Trattoria Omero – a must whenever he would visit. There we would gorge on typical

Tuscan fare: pappardelle with hare sauce, penne strascicate or fried rabbit with courgette. It was always lovely to have lunch with him – finally, he would devote some time to me. Not to mention, he had those funny Anglo-Tuscan ways that so amused me. Even his way of dressing was totally original. I remember him wearing a yellow tie with an emerald green jacket, colours only he could wear.

When he was in Italy, he felt British and – speaking a mixture of English and Italian – would criticise the shortcomings of Italians. Yet, when in Britain, he felt Italian and loved upsetting the phlegmatic British in his rapid-fire English and with the jaw-dropping speed at which we so recklessly drove.

Time and again, he captivated me with his stories – with their mix of fantasy and truth – and his projects for the future. He wanted to go to Jordan and buy a horse from King Hussein, start a foundation for young aspiring leather goods manufacturers that would be named after him, buy purebred pigeons in Reggio Emilia or waxbills in Africa, and maybe even own a castle in Scotland. He was bursting with ideas.

It left me spellbound, yet I would have liked him to have paid more attention to me sometimes. Daughters expect total approval from their fathers but with him, reassurances and support never came freely. I had to deserve them. What's more, his reactions were jarring. He would go from never asking me any questions, making me think he hadn't noticed me, or else would recall every single detail and peremptorily give me orders.

About a fortnight after that last visit, we received a telephone call from his secretary, Angela, informing us that my father had been rushed to hospital. He had fallen into a coma.

My mother, my sister and I tried desperately to catch the first plane to London. In spite of all the difficulties throughout their marriage and their long separation, my mother wanted to be there for his last farewell, casting aside her discomfort at being amongst strangers. Her desire to give him a good send-off was much too strong, despite everything that had transpired.

Alas, we arrived a day too late so could only visit him in the morgue. Seeing him like that, I froze. While my mother and sister went to give him a final kiss, I stood there stock still, staring at him.

I touched his hand, which was cold to the touch and upset me so much that I was completely immobilised, unable to lean in closer and give him one last kiss as well.

Uncle Giorgio, the brother who was most devoted to him and who had understood him best, also came to the funeral, having arrived from Rome the day prior. It struck me a lot that, during the ceremony and the beginning of the "tribute", as is common practice in Anglo-Saxon countries, Giorgio began to cry almost to the point of hysterics, having lost a brother, one who was rebellious and difficult but who also showed his true affections.

Out of all the brothers, Uncle Giorgio had been in much more frequent touch with father in recent years. Roberto did not even go to the funeral, turning up only for the burial in Italy's Porto San Stefano at Argentario.

But on that occasion, Roberto was certainly upset. My uncle was quite skilled at holding back his emotions but he was also very tense due to the presence of a number of photographers and journalists whose presence was truly uncalled for on that particular occasion.

The funeral took place in the small parish church of Rusper. The coffin arrived on a black hearse pulled by two black horses with plumes on their heads, driven by a coachman in a top hat and formal uniform. My sister Elizabeth, Penny (my father's companion) and I followed in a car behind.

Throughout the brief ride to the church, we sat in an unreal silence which seemed to echo through my bones.

As is custom in Anglo-Saxon countries, after the service we went to his house for cocktails. I did not join the others but instead went to my father 's study and cried with Thinky, his dog. Thinky was a saluki, a greyhound whose lineage extends back to ancient Egypt. They are especially suited to living together with horses. Indeed, a horse breeder had given Thinky to my father. Watching Thinky race alongside the horses in the fields of the stud farm was always exhilarating. When he spotted a hare, he would immediately point at it with a raised paw, standing perfectly still except for some twitching, continue to point until he was ready to pounce. By then, the hare was inevitably long gone.

In the study, I felt defeated and in disbelief. I just couldn't accept the thought of never seeing my father again and the pain tore me apart. All my life, I had sought to establish a calm and balanced relationship with him - I had almost managed to do so and now his death had upended everything.

Paolo Gucci was buried in the cemetery of Porto Santo Stefano, on the Argentario peninsula, alongside his mother, Olwen Price. Uncle Giorgio owned a fine house nearby, where both my father and grandma had often enjoyed a relaxing getaway.

On the coffin lay a rough wooden cross, the gift of a fellow prisoner. About a year earlier, my father had spent twenty days in a detention centre in the U.S.A. for failing to respond to the unreasonable financial demands of his alleged English wife, Jenny, whom he had married unlawfully in Haiti (since my father was not yet legally separated from my mother).

I, too, wanted to leave him a departing gift – an envelope containing a letter to send him off on his last journey. I have always believed that the physical journey of this life has a beginning and an end, but our soul, our energy, lives on. Thus, that letter would ensure a continuation of our dialogue in the peaceful realm beyond life on earth. The dead remain by our side.

Sometime later, I came to realise that I did not know how my father died. Indeed, I still do not know. Why did his wait so long to take him to hospital, given that he had been ill for some days? Why had she not taken him earlier to shorten his suffering at home? Why had she waited until the last moment to bundle him into the car and drive him to the hospital, taking all that time that could have been spent saving his life, finally arriving only when my father was falling into a coma?

Setting these memories and thoughts down on paper is my way of continuing my dialogue with my father. I came to realise that this was how I could acknowledge my great debt to this controversial figure, this man I both doted on and despised, yet whose greatness I cannot fail to recognise. Now, I understand how important he has been to me throughout my life.

My parents get married

———

P aolo Gucci and Yvonne Moschetto first crossed paths one afternoon in Rome in 1949. They were at a party hosted by Danilo, a mutual friend. My father immediately noticed the attractive girl whilst Yvonne sensed somebody gazing at her intently. The party finished early and my mother went home. On that occasion, they were not able to talk to each other, however Paolo later managed to get her address. A few days later, looking out of her bedroom window, she spotted the fair-haired lad she had seen at the party. He was sitting on a bench in the small square in front of her house. He had been looking up at her window for hours. Over the next three days, Paolo would return again and again to sit on that same bench. It would have been unthinkable for Yvonne to go downstairs and talk to a stranger in that manner. My mother, born into a family of aristocrats and military officers, had been brought up quite strictly.

Indeed, her father, Riccardo Moschetto, came from a distinguished family in Palermo. My Nonna Carlotta, born in Trieste when the city was still part of the Austro-Hungarian Empire, had met Riccardo, a lieutenant in the Italian Army, during World War I. In 1925, his elder brother – a Navy officer and commander of Tobruk harbour in Libya – called him to come and manage the Savings Bank of Derna. Riccardo was later transferred with his family to Bengasi, where he became Director General of the Savings Bank there. When World War II broke out in 1940, he was drafted back into the army and put on the front lines in Tobruk.

At the end of the war, Riccardo retreated with his troops to Tripoli, where he fell gravely ill. For two years, his family had no news from him. On his return to Italy, the supreme military tribunal in Rome declared him a war invalid. He died a few years later in the Italian capital. His coffin was escorted by an honour guard.

But returning back to the young man in the park, Yvonne thought it strange that that he should sit out there instead of going to her father and formally introducing himself. A few months later, though, she received a letter from England.

Delighted, she opened the envelope and recognised the signature as the name of the young man at the party – the one who Danilo had later identified for her. Intrigued, Yvonne read the letter. Paolo was writing to her from his mother Olwen's house in Wales, where he spent his summers after the end of the school year. His romantic and impassioned tone won her over. Paolo confessed that from the first moment he had laid eyes her, he had been unable to stop thinking about her. He openly declared his torment at not being able to see her, and longed to do so. They must meet in Rome when he got back, in Piazza dei Giudici at 3:00 pm on 6th October. Paolo followed this up with a dramatic declaration that if she did not come, he would commit suicide.

My mother was upset by Paolo's assertion and sought advice from Sergio, a friend and schoolmate. Should she go to the appointment? Finally, without telling her family, she decided that yes, she would go.

Paolo showed up dressed in perfect British style, wearing a tweed jacket, brown trousers and a green ascot with blue stripes around the neck. Only later did Yvonne discover that for his dates with her, Paolo blithely borrowed clothes from his father Aldo's wardrobe. He famously sported long hair when this was not yet in style. The Principal of Paolo's school, the Collegio Nazareno, often threatened both him and his inseparable friend, Prince Raimondo Orsini, that they would not be allowed to attend classes with such an unsightly hairdo.

Paolo and Yvonne's first meeting proved somewhat awkward. My father was emotional and talked about all sorts of things, including himself, his life and the unhappy atmosphere at home due to his parents' difficult relationship.

Alas, my grandparents did not get on very well. They had constant quarrels, maybe because Aldo was Florentine and Olwen British, two cultures that are quite different indeed. Aldo, moreover, was a strict disciplinarian; he did not like his children loafing around and made them work in the Gucci shop on Via Condotti from a young age.

Paolo told Yvonne he had just turned eighteen. Only later did my mother discover that he was only seventeen, and so a year her junior. Paolo's handsome looks, blue eyes, elegance and charming ways did not leave her unimpressed. Yvonne herself was quite beautiful: she was unique, feminine and unsophisticated – people even said she resembled Catherine Deneuve.

Following their first date, Paolo and Yvonne met several times again. They would take walks, often along Via Veneto. Paolo was very religious at that time so took her to a church where they met his friend, Father Antonio.

Once they walked past the Bocca della Verità, an ancient marble mask under the portico of the Church of Santa Maria in Cosmedin. Tradition has it that if you put your hand in its mouth and lie, it will bite you. With her hand inside the mouth, my father made my mother swear she would never leave him.

Grandfather Aldo was not only passionate about fashion but sports cars as well. On country outings, Paolo would drive his father's beautiful red 1100 Stanguellini, a special make of sports cars manufactured in Modena in the 1930s. Obviously, he would borrow it without his father knowing. Once they had an unforgettable trip to Ostia, by the sea. Paolo showed up with Kim, his black Great Dane, sitting in the back seat of Aldo's enchanting green convertible Austin Healey. The day passed happily, with the pair enjoying a picnic on the beach, a dip in the water and a lovely sunset. On the way back, owing to my father's spirited driving, as they careered downhill around a bend, they skidded off the road and landed on top of a house beneath the overhang. Luckily nobody was injured. My mother only had a bump on her forehead which she took great pains to conceal under her wavy blonde hair when she returned home. But the car was quite banged up. A contrite Paolo knew he would have a hard time explaining this one to his father. So, he rang his friend Danilo Oddi, asking him for advice.

The next day at school, my mother told her friend Adriana Mordasini, daughter of the Swiss Consul in Rome, about the previous day's mishap, begging her to keep it secret. But things did not go smoothly. Adriana went home and related the story to her own mother, who happened to be a friend of Nonna Carlotta.

When my mother arrived home, her father Riccardo was waiting for her. "What have you been up to?

Are you still seeing that Paolo fellow?" Evidently, he knew what had happened and was angrily demanding an explanation from his daughter.

"I hope you realise that we know absolutely nothing about this boy. He is not properly educated yet says he owns a shop. He is not the right kind of person for you, nor for our family."

Yet, in spite of her parents' opposition, Yvonne continued seeing Paolo. Knowing what a passion Paolo had for animals, she once even gave him a hawk. She had purchased this rare specimen from Mendillo's, a well-known shop on Via della Mercede.

The Gucci house was always full of animals. In addition to Kim, there was Rongo – also a Great Dane but white in colour – who belonged to Uncle Roberto.

In return for her gift, Paolo gave Yvonne a small onyx ring, which my mother cherished all throughout her life.

The two continued dating in secret. To see Paolo, Yvonne would head out with her sister Giovanna, then part ways at the first street corner. Other times, Yvonne would seek help from their mutual friend Danilo Oddi, who knew about their liaison.

During their long courtship, Yvonne broke up with Paolo on three occasions, always due to family disagreements. The Moschetto family considered the Guccis to be simple merchants, shop proprietors, and wanted a better suitor for their daughter.

Paolo took advantage of their time apart to finish his secondary school education. His father sent him to a boarding school in Genoa. From there, he wrote dozens of passionate letters to my mother, telling her how much he missed her. My mother answered, all the while trying to keep a level head.

Paolo returned to Rome in 1953. By this time, he was sending my mother telegrams as well as letters. I once came across one of them. He writes: "As you awake, think how very very much I love you. Paolo."

New Year's Eve of 1950 has gone down in family lore. Yvonne was not allowed to go out that night and this upset Paolo greatly. Just before midnight, he crossed the entire length and breadth of Rome, from Via Condotti to Via Lago di Lesina, with two glasses and a bottle of champagne in hand.

When he reached Yvonne's house, he started throwing pebbles up at her window. She saw him and rushed downstairs, where they welcomed in the new year with a toast. Then he raced back home quickly, with no-one the wiser.

Paolo and Yvonne took lots of walks in the Borghese gardens, before taking a seat on a bench to look over the drawings each had done. Both had an artistic streak but their sketches were different: my father's were original and extravagant whilst my mother's works were more classic.

Finally, during a trip to Lugano, on a romantic path around the lake and in the stillness of that enchanted location, Paolo asked Yvonne to marry him. She very happily said yes.

The wedding took place in Rome – the city where they had first met – in the Church of Santa Francesca Romana, near the Colosseum. The ceremony was simple and officiated by Father Antonio, in the presence of the bride and bridegroom's parents (who had finally come around) and some friends.

After their honeymoon in Lugano, Paolo and Yvonne went to live in Florence, on Corso Italia. Those were quiet, untroubled years for both the business and the family. During this time, two daughters were born – my elder sister Elisabetta and I.

My childhood in Florence

Memory's voice wells up from the heart and helps us remember.

I spent my childhood in Florence. We lived in the house that had belonged to my great grandmother Aida, wife of Guccio, the founder of the Gucci dynasty. It was a two-storey townhouse with garden at Via della Farina 45, with a tall magnolia that is still visible today from the street.

The house on Via della Farina was always an important base for our family, for this was where my great grandfather Guccio had lived.

It was a luxurious home for those times. One the ground level were the master quarters. The front door opened onto a large entryway embellished by a red carpet. This was where we usually had our tree at Christmas.

One year my mother invited our cousins – Uncle Roberto's children – to spend the Christmas holidays with us. Wishing to treat us with a big surprise, she invited *zampognari*, the celebrated Italian-style bagpipe players from southern Italy, to come play for us. While we children were all gathered around the tree unwrapping our gifts, the bell rang. Three tall, rigid-looking men with huge bellies came in and started playing their bagpipes. Their music was so loud and raucous in the large entrance hall, that we children were frightened and started bawling. Thus, a lovely surprise home concert ended in tears. Unhappily, my mother had to ask the bagpipe players to leave.

The entryway led into the dining room and the large living room, with its combo radio-record player. Here, I would listen to my favourite music, such as Yves Montand's song Abat-Jour, which I loved also for its wonderful rhythm. Even though I couldn't understand French at that time, the language has never ceased to fascinate me.

From the hall you reached the studio which had a TV set and a bookcase full of all the cups my father had won with his carrier pigeons.

On the same ground floor were the bedrooms. Elisabetta and I had a room to ourselves. We took advantage of this to bounce like mad things on the beds when we were alone. Given our strict upbringing, we were expected to be in bed and fast asleep by 9:00 p.m.

Yet, the two of us would sneak out of our room on all fours and head for the studio, where the grownups would sit chatting around the TV. We would watch and listen, intrigued.

The children's playroom was past the kitchen. This was where we girls could give free rein to our imagination.

Elisabetta, being the elder sister, held the sceptre of command. She decided what games we played and I deferred to her. This was the rule. She could be quite mischievous, though, and often took advantage of my much milder, more yielding character.

Dolls did not particularly interest us but we loved playing at being teachers or salesgirls. We would invent names and take our roles seriously, as though it were all true.

Our favourite pastime in the garden was a game played with a hula hoop. I usually lost, while my sister always worked hard to win.

As the first granddaughter in the family, Elisabetta was pampered a lot – much more than I ever was. Over the years, our positions changed: when we started going to school, I excelled in studies while Elisabetta only just scraped by.

One day, someone gave us a live chick. We called him Pio and would secretly take him to bed with us at night, taking turns at cuddling him under the sheets.

Thereafter, we always came back from school with just one thought on our minds: where was our chick? We would call him in a loud voice: "Pio, Pio," and again, "Pio, Pio..." Finally, his little yellow head would pop out from somewhere.

The gardener, we realised, had started complaining that the flower and leaf buds on his plants were our darling Pio's favourite food. A few days later, our usual call "Pio, Pio!" was met with silence. We looked for him in vain all over the garden, finally resigning ourselves to the fact that Pio had grown up and was now gone ...

I would say the gardener did it but I dare not think of how or where.

On the ground floor of the house was the famous billiard room. The family played pool there almost every Sunday, with all my uncles and my grandfather joining in. Some of the men would smoke pipes, others cigars, so that the billiard room would soon grow thick with smoke. My Uncle Rodolfo's wife, Alessandra, often joined the men in their games. Thanks to her German origins, she had a strong character. This constantly put her at loggerheads with my grandfather, Aldo. She always played to win, exactly like "Daddy", as my grandfather insisted we use in addressing him.

Nanna Olwen did not play but would wait patiently for Alessandra to finish her game. Afterwards, they would go for a stroll in the garden, speaking only in English. This gave them sense of unity, being both foreigners in Italy.

The billiard table, whose surface was entirely inlaid, also served as a hiding place for Christmas presents. This is how one fine day I discovered that our gifts did not come from Santa Claus but rather materialised from under the billiard table!

In the rack hanging on the wall stood the cues. Each player had his own, with his initials engraved in ivory on the wooden handle. The cue belonging to my great grandfather Guccio Gucci, who died before I was born, had passed down to my Uncle Vasco, Grandfather Aldo's brother.

Then there was Aldo's cue, and those belonging to Rodolfo, my grandfather's younger brother, and to my father. Vasco, Aldo and my father used to have great games, while smoking Tuscan cigars and discussing business matters.

Right from the beginning grandfather Aldo distinguished himself in the family with his charisma and his authority over his offspring. He would let no opportunity to put his strong personality and enormous determination on display pass by. Indeed, he was a fascinating man and this always aided him in promoting his ideas and personal views. Aldo would not suffer being contradicted and accepted advice only from very few people. Once he had made a decision, there was no going back on it. Aldo, as I remember, regarded his children as being one step below him. As the years went by, this side of his character changed – not for the better, it only became more complex.

Regretfully, I missed the chance of getting to know my grandfather as well as I would have liked. He lived in the U.S., so there was little chance of our meeting. What's more, he was a man who devoted most of his time to his work. For him, family came second.

For us girls, the billiard room, with its marble floor and brightly lit window overlooking the garden, was a place to hide when Signora Ines came round to give us injections. The large green armchair in the corner served this purpose best. It always took Emma and Pina, our two nannies, half an hour or more to find me, after they had searched everywhere in the house. Only then, frightened and tearful, would I come out and surrender.

Emma looked after us all day. She was rather chubby, gathered her hair in a bun at the back of her head and wore a huge white apron. I remember how once, when she was preparing minestrone in one of our first pressure cookers, the cooker exploded, sending courgettes, carrots and string beans flying, even sticking to the kitchen walls. Still today, pressure cookers scare me.

Pina was our nanny for many years. Having originally come

from Istria with my maternal Nonna Carlotta, she had served the Moschetto family both in Bengasi and Rome, had raised my mother and after my parents had married, lived with her in Florence. I, too, grew up and became a teenager under her watchful gaze. Pina, who was in our service for more than fifty years, was an amazing woman – strong, determined, loving and a great cook all rolled into one.

The dishes Pina cooked were evidence of my family's composite origins. She had learned to make Apfelstrudel from Nonna Carlotta, while she prepared rice pudding according to Nanna Olwen's recipe. Then there was English-style roast beef with Worcestershire sauce, Tuscan-style rabbit and Sicilian cassata, which were Grandfather Riccardo's favourites.

I can't recall Daddy ever getting emotional. My mother told me that perhaps the only time it happened was when Elisabetta was born. She was his first granddaughter. When mother and child came home from the hospital, Daddy expressly asked my mother to let the baby sleep in his own bed.

The request left everyone astounded, as they had always thought him a tough man, averse to displaying his feelings. The following day, this aspect of his character was confirmed: "Yvonne, last night Elisabetta cried non-stop. I didn't get a wink of sleep so I will gladly return her to you!"

My father Paolo was very exacting at the dinner table. Everything had to be just right. He expected the plates to be quite hot and was so fastidious that if a dish had not been cooked to perfection, he would rush to the kitchen and complain. Only on important occasions were we girls allowed to eat at the table with the grownups: my father thought children should eat in the kitchen until they learned proper table manners. So, my sister and I sadly ate our butterfly-shaped pasta sitting at a small table in a corner of the kitchen. Maybe it was just as well, for when I did grow up a little and was allowed to sit at the table with my elders, my father turned out to be exceedingly strict, with dinner often ending in tragedy. He would make a special point that I finish all the food on my plate, keep my elbows down and not play with my bread. A nightmare.

The garden of our Florence house had a large aviary full of homing pigeons. My father spent hours and hours with them, often ending up with a feather or two in his hair, which would make me laugh.

His passion for birds had begun early in life. He started out with hawks then went on to purebred pigeons, and finally to homing pigeons. In his infinite passion for homing pigeons, he did almost maniacal things. He even started a club in Florence – the 'Colombofili in Italia' – of which he became president. As time passed, he became famous but still took great pleasure in organising competitions and even creating the medals and cups that they would present to the winners, which he would often win himself.

One day, rummaging through a box, I found hundreds of medals, certificates and cups that he had collected over the years and which he guarded meticulously in his study. He subscribed to magazines from all over the world specialising in homing pigeons, in which he passionately read everything there was to know about them, from wingspan to their unique eyes and red or burgundy claws. He managed to travel to America just to go and see a particular breed of pigeons – perhaps famous for their speed – and obviously to buy a pair to breed with his own.

In a van he had purchased for this particular passion of his, he would transport the birds to various destinations across Italy, where he released them for their return flight. Each bird had a ring fastened to its leg. As soon as it returned to the aviary, the ring was removed and placed in a special device that calculated the minutes and seconds of its time of arrival. The owner of the fastest pigeon won the competition. But my father had a secret: when he saw the pigeon alight on the roof of the aviary, he would whistle to it, with some feed in his hand, to make it descend faster.

At one point, my father went to live for some time in New York and even there, he had a dovecote built on the terrace of his penthouse, with the poor things fluttering about amongst the skyscrapers.

But it was in England where he would eventually create the largest dovecote, totalling some four hundred pigeons.

The garden also had a fishpond, assiduously frequented by all the neighbourhood cats, who never knew whether to go for the pigeons or the goldfish.

Eventually, he decided that the "era of homing pigeons" had to end, not least because he grew allergic to the feathers which would cause him to become strangely feverish. Hence, after even trying to visit the dovecote with a gas mask on, he realised that in addition to frightening the birds, he simply could not continue to keep them.

So, he moved on to Arabian horses! There too he spent hours and hours, ofttimes with me present so he could show me hundreds of slides, to look at the tail, held high in a certain way, the various lengths of the neck, the coat.

In the stables, he would play music or turn on the radio because he said it was good for the horses' mood. In their stables, each horse had its own blanket bearing the name of the horse and "Stable PG" embroidered on it. Even the saddles were the result of much study and detailed work, always in black and red. He was able to buy the most famous (and of course, the most expensive) Arabian horses. Once he had an idea in his mind, it was difficult to convince him otherwise.

It was also at that time that he created a beautiful scarf adorned with rosettes that were given to winners of the various competitions. It was a true masterpiece. That scarf was not from the Gucci collection but by Paolo Gucci.

Even my father's hobbies prove that he was certainly a unique person.

Whenever we would go to the mountains, if you were to suggest going for a walk, he would eventually look up and say,

"I'm going to that point there. You go back and I'll come and join you in an hour."

Once in Canazei, in the Dolomites, while we were there on holiday, we waited for him for hours after a walk. As evening came without him returning, we called the forester before heading out in search for him along the path we had taken towards the highest peak of the mountain. We came across him as darkness was falling, totally calm. He was adventurous but also somewhat irresponsible. He didn't think much about the consequences of anything and he certainly did not lack courage.

Overall, I recall my childhood as being a peaceful time. I was a quiet child, even though loquacious upon occasions, especially when we went for family outings to Rome to visit my grandmother. The moment we set off, I would start talking about this and that while looking out of the window: school, my schoolmates, homework, my many dreams, including my great passion for Rome, where I wanted to live. My father would exclaim, "My, what a chatterbox you are!" Then we played our favourite game: I would say a letter and all of us had to find as many words as possible beginning with that letter.

I didn't see my father much – he always worked right up to dinnertime then when he returned home, he was tired and irritable. And I was likely already in bed. Sometimes, he would make an appearance in our room, reprimanding us in a severe tone if we had been caught getting up to some mischief. Whenever that happened, I always pretended I was asleep.

From nursery school through middle school, I went to an English institution in Florence's Santa Reparata, run by the Blue Sisters. It was the same school my father and his brothers had attended during their childhood. I wore a black smock and a white collar, which Pina washed and ironed to perfection. I enjoyed my studies and earnt high marks, sometimes even top marks. The Blue Sisters were kind and lots of fun. They wore somewhat shorter skirts and of course I, like all my schoolmates, had that irresistible wish to pull off their veil and see their hair. They taught us to sing "God Save the Queen" and when I got especially good marks, they would invite me for tea, which would be served with classical music playing in the background.

Christmas letters to my father and mother had to be in English. Mine included a wish list of the presents I desired. I would promise not to quarrel with my sister anymore and to follow all the rules. The last wish I would note down was always to spend more time with my father.

I loved going to school. The moment I heard the horn of the school bus sounding outside our house, I would rush out, with my school cap on my head. The only thing I found boring was high mass every morning before classes started, which used to last so long.

Our house on via della Camilluccia in Rome

In 1952 my grandparents Aldo and Olwen, who lived in Rome, relocated from their apartment on Via Condotti, above the Gucci shop, to a house in Monte Mario that Aldo had built specially for them. It was a luxurious villa with a swimming pool and two great palm trees standing at either side of the steps paved with cobblestones that led up to it. In front of the swimming pool was a shed painted red, surrounded by pink bougainvillea bushes. Here, we changed into our bathing suit.

A long tree-lined drive ended in a marble staircase leading up to the front door. Inside the house were small sitting rooms. The one I liked best contained a piano and a fireplace. Grandfather Aldo played both the piano and the viola da gamba well; he would call us children into the room and we would listen to him enraptured. In later years, his concerts grew few and far between, as he was far too busy working.

The whole house smelled deliciously of the wax that was used to polish the wood flooring.

Some scents you never forget.

Near the main house was a greenhouse full of old and new children's playthings, including roller skates, hula hoops, a swing, various handcarts and a rocking chair. We kids loved splashing around in the swimming pool and having diving competitions. The water was always cold and it would take us a while before deciding to jump in. One late summer afternoon, grandfather

Aldo came out and saw us sitting by the water. "Why aren't you in the pool on such a hot day?" "The water is freezing cold!" "What nonsense..." he exclaimed. Tossing off his bathrobe, he dived straight into the water. Now, that was a good lesson in character!

For Christmas dinner, the whole family would assemble at my grandparents' house: my father Paolo and his brothers Roberto and Giorgio with their wives, and all eleven cousins.

A vast Christmas tree stood in the great hall with its mahogany floor. A flight of stairs, also in mahogany, led upstairs. From here, we could get within reach of the top of the tree, where the gift for the youngest grandchild would hang. The grand finale was a delicious Christmas pudding flambé.

My grandmother Olwen – "Nanna", as we grandchildren called her – was English. As mentioned, in her early days, she had been a lady-in-waiting to Queen Helen of Romania, living in the Villa Sparta in Fiesole, a hill-top town near Florence, before meeting her husband in the first Gucci shop in Florence, who she married in Wales in 1927.

Olwen Price, daughter of George Price, was born in Wales in November 1908. Typically British, she was fair-haired, blue-eyed and very sweet. Her father owned a factory of horse carriages in Shrewsbury. Olwen managed not only to have class but also be an uncomplicated woman.

She wore sober-coloured suits, a string of pearls and sported a Gucci handbag at all times. As with all English people, she was passionately attached to her native land. Her Italian was not very good, even after she had lived in the country for forty years. I shall always remember her struggling with certain words: "Dobbiamo far riverniciare la panchina *veerrdeh*". We would laugh and correct her: "Nanna, it's pronounced 'verde'!"

Nanna Olwen was also typically English in her love for animals. She had two Yorkshire Terriers and three Persian tabby cats, with which she spent long hours. This breed of cats was well known for being very shy. Every time I visited my grandmother in Rome, they would vanish behind the furniture. I waited in vain for them to come out from under a chest of drawers, so that we could play. The loveliest memory I have of my Nanna is of her sitting in her armchair in front of the lighted fireplace, surrounded by her house pets. Then, at 5:00 pm on the dot, in came tea and biscuits.

Other fond memories relate to our farewells. She used to stand at the front door, at the top of the stairs, with big tears in her eyes. It was the same thing when we went to mass at the Church of Santa Chiara near Ponte Milvio – as soon as the organ started playing, she couldn't hold back the waterworks.

After a typical English breakfast of porridge, ham, bacon and eggs, she would open the window and whistle to a robin redbreast she knew. The little fellow would come and perch on her hand, eating the breadcrumbs she held in her palm.

Olwen was a mild, sensitive, generous person. She adored her grandchildren and lived for us, knitted cardigans and gave us lots of presents. I still have some today. When returning from a visit to England, she brought us chocolate with raisins. I particularly remember two beautiful blue raincoats with a plaid lining – her gift to my sister and me. Olwen had bought them a few sizes too large, saying that in this way they would last longer. Sometimes we had to wait a year or more before we could wear her gifts!

Nanna Olwen was my refuge. She always had a consoling word when I was upset; then she would hold my hand in hers and tell me how much she loved me. Her life wasn't easy, what with the difficult relationship with Aldo and the family's ups and downs. When arguments flared up between my father and my grandfather, she would interrupt them and, with her British aplomb, ask: "Would you like a cup of tea?" I always admired that typically-English detachment of hers.

During the war and the ensuing German occupation of Italy, my grandmother kept in touch with an English priest at the San Carlo Church in Rome. He would ask her to hide Royal Air Force officers in her house and she obliged. The family then lived on

Via Condotti, above the Gucci shop. My father remembered a Scottish pilot hiding in the attic who on occasions would get a little tipsy and start singing at the top of his lungs. Nanna had to rush upstairs to tell him in no uncertain terms how dangerous his behaviour was.

During my time in Cambridge, I spent two months in the home of Mr Lesley, one of my grandmother's wartime protégés. He played the piano wonderfully. Remembering his time in Rome, tears would gleam in his eyes.

After the war, Olwen was awarded a special badge of merit by General HR Alexander for having saved the lives of British Commonwealth soldiers. She never gave a thought to the danger she was in, driven by her courage and deep love for her beloved homeland.

Her husband, Aldo – Daddy – was not very good at being a grandfather. Above all, he was a brilliant and far-sighted businessman, considering the Gucci company to be his real family. With us, Aldo laid down the law – we must do as he says. In any case, opposing such a strong character would have been useless. I felt shy in his presence, hardly daring to open my mouth.

Yet in spite of Aldo's brusque manner, he would often give us grandchildren a prototype of each new Gucci creation and an envelope with some money in it.

Like all the men of the Gucci family, he was also a charmer, born to seduce, and had a decidedly weak spot for women. He had a distinctive look, with his elegance and his refinement, his cuff-links and a foulard in his breast pocket.

Every year, we went to Versilia for the summer holidays – first to Forte dei Marmi and later to Ronchi, where we stayed in the so-called "Casa Bianca", a villa belonging to Aunt Drusilla and her husband Uncle Roberto. How great it was to open the chest containing our summer wardrobe. There were lots of frills and white collars and a wonderful smell of freshly-washed garments. We would leave Rome in June – my mother, my sister, our nanny Pina and I. My father joined us on weekends. Sometimes, when he came, we had great picnics. We used to pack dishes, forks and cups in a lovely Gucci basket made of flower-patterned jute.

We had a set routine. Mornings were spent with our mother and our nanny at Bagno Rosina, where we swam for hours. Then we went home for lunch. After a short nap, back we went to the beach. Later in the afternoon, we would ride our bicycles to Ronchi to meet our cousins, Roberto's children, as well as our cousins from Scamacca.

We were a big group of kids of roughly the same age and really enjoyed playing together. A favourite pastime was the cardboard house, which we had built all by ourselves. It even had a door and a window. This was our hideout of choice.

Sometimes in the afternoon we went to Valè's to binge on *schiacciatine* – mini focaccias.

In the mornings at Bagno Rosa, we each had a friend along with us – Gabriella, Ginevra and Sabina. Sometimes boys came along too and it always seemed as if they took turns in courting either my sister or me.

One day on the beach I met Andrea. I was given special permission to go the movies with him. We went to the first evening showing at an open-air cinema. I noticed that throughout the film, he was looking more at me than at the screen. Then Andrea took my hand and as far as I was concerned ... we were as good as engaged!

Those childhood summer vacations were happy times. I had five cousins to play with: Cosimo, Filippo, Uberto, Olimpia and Domitilla. We brought our bicycles from Florence and all of us girls would go on long rides along the seafront and under the pines. It was so nice to go back to the same friends every year – girls and boys my own age. When I turned thirteen, my parents finally allowed me to go to the celebrated Capannina, a club where you could dance all night. But I had to be home by eleven – just when things got exciting! And always accompanied by my sister.

One day, my father showed up with a new purchase. It was an 8-metre, all-white Owens cabin cruiser with wooden interior, which for those times was a real luxury. He called it the Ennovy – my mother's name written backwards.

I was maybe seven or eight years old. As always, my father choice his vessel very carefully, then decked it out meticulously. I remember that everything was blue and red, from the tablecloths to the sheets and the porcelain plates that bore the name of the boat. He even had two beautiful Gucci table lamps made – one with a blue leather base bearing a barometer and the other with an anchor applied to the leather base.

Many trips were taken on that boat. It was moored in the Port of Carrara, hence our destinations were the Apuan Riviera, Portofino and the Ligurian coast.

It was fun to swim and hang out with my father but our outings on the Ennovy became increasingly challenging given that my father was an obsessive and picky captain. "Don't sit there, you'll get the cushions wet ... don't come on board with your shoes on ... dry yourself immediately after swimming ... don't walk around when the boat is moving ... clean this ... put the matt there." Our miniature cruises to wonderful places became a tormenting list of dos and don'ts.

Sometimes we were joined by Nanna Olwen and Aunt Giovanna, my mother's sister. One day, we were sailing along and everything was just fine when my Nanna and Aunt started whispering to us, "We're seasick ..." Fearful of annoying our father, we answered: "Come on, you'll be alright," only to watch them grow paler by the minute. As we were approaching Bocca di Magra, we told our father. Without batting an eyelid, he turned the boat around and headed straight back for Punta Bianca. There he plopped them down on a rock while we continued our cruise and had fun diving off the side of the boat. An hour later, we returned to collect the two ladies and went home.

I remember that Uncle Roberto also bought the exact same boat and named it "Noi Cinque". At the time, he only had three children, so there were five ("cinque") of them in the family, with another yet to be born. Indeed, some time later he bought an even bigger boat.

We also often went out with Uncle Roberto. But it was exactly the same on his boat – you never knew where to move. In the end, these trips proved more exhausting than relaxing!

Via delle Caldaie

In the afternoon, whenever I had no homework, I would visit my father at the Gucci processing plant on Via delle Caldaie. On Saturdays, my father and I would bicycle to the Gucci shop on Via della Vigna Nuova, where we always had lots of fun. I would have been around eight or nine years old. The establishment on Via delle Caldaie was our second, having been purchased by Guccio in 1951. Our first site, on Lungarno Guicciardini, I only saw in later years. Upon arrival, I would immediately head upstairs to the modellers' department on the second floor. Climbing up on a tall stool in front of the workbench, my legs dangling down, I would rest my head in my hands and watch the modellers working busily away. It was truly mesmerising.

The modeller Mario prepared and cut new forms for women's purses – first in cardboard, then in a special cloth called salpa, and finally in the leather he and my father had selected together.

A special leather that became a hallmark of the Gucci lines – a sampling of matelassé pigskin, called brindle – had actually resulted from a mistake.

My grandfather had gone to a tannery in Scotland. The people there brought out the pigskin samples they had prepared for him. One of these, they apologetically pointed out, was spoiled and full of tiny stains. Aldo looked at it, looked again, and finally exclaimed that it had an original and beautiful finish, and was indeed a most fortunate mistake! He placed orders for it, intending to use it for suitcases and purses.

Going from one workbench to another, I would witness the magic birth of Gucci handbags. To my great wonder, a wooden cut-out of the purse, just received from the carpentry department, would end up on the modeller's table. Once the purse had been cut out, it was entrusted to the delicate hands of the seamstresses, who sewed it into one piece in such an original and painstaking manner that the stitching itself became one of the hallmarks of Gucci manufacturing. For the final touch, bamboo was heated over a flame to be bent into the famous Gucci handle shape. Still produced today, this handle was originally based on Uncle Vasco's collection of walking sticks.

Uncle Vasco didn't only collect walking sticks: he also had a passion for antique objects, which he picked up on his frequent trips to London and all over the world, from the USA to South America. He bought everything that struck his fancy and took it back to Florence. These objects first served him as inspiration for new gift items. Then they became part of his private collection of antiques, which he kept in his office above the Gucci shop in Florence.

My uncle loved plays and often went to the theatre. When he was too busy, he passed on the tickets to one of his shop assistants. Vasco was an extremely sociable person, and with the excuse of organising hunting parties, he invited Florence's high society to lavish banquets that he hosted at his country home.

Like all Guccis, my uncle had a great sense of humour. But his straightforwardness distinguished him from the rest of the family. He was very direct in both his professional and personal relationships, yet always attentive to the needs of others and displaying his humanity.

Finally, I would watch a worker at the end of the line embossing a number inside the handbag and recording the name of the bag's creator so that it could be traced back to them in the event of any defects. Then, they placed a lovely little mirror, carefully wrapped in tissue paper, inside the bag's inner pocket. And here it was, the famous 0633, first created in 1947.

How excited I was to see that same purse displayed in the window of our Via della Vigna Nuova store!

My father would let me play with the leather cuttings. This is how I developed the ability to recognise that particular smell of leather which even today, when I enter a workshop, takes me back to those days. In an attic above the workshop was a shelf with small drawers crammed with accessories for handbags: buttons, clasps, handles and clips. Every now and then, my father would call me in and say in his usual severe tone: "Take a tray, go upstairs and bring me down some samples of clasps set with stones." I would head off with some trepidation and choose the right pieces from amongst the large quantity of objects. But I would be distracted playing with the objects and losing all track of time, only to scolded by my father when I finally returned.

Other times, I would slip into the room where the beige-coloured cardboard models were kept. Each bore its own number and hung from a hook. I longed to touch them but knew I couldn't.

One time in that room, I saw my father sniff at a piece of leather and enquired, "What are you doing?"

He explained that leather has a particular odour that is a guarantee of its originality. Just then, Mario the modeller walked in and took those two crescent-shaped pieces of beige cardboard.

That was how I saw the 1244 Half Moon handbag come into being under my very eyes. Soft and loose, with a broad shoulder-strap and a cylindrical snap-hook on the front, it became a Gucci bestseller. The handbag was also produced in deerskin, a true innovation at the time.

Later, I learned that the Countess Agusta, a famous client of ours, had wanted the purse to be soft, not stiff. While I listened on, Signor Luigi Limberti came in. An old supplier for Gucci – having worked with us since the 1960s – he had two lovely white bags with him, one in calfskin and the other in saffiano leather. I recognised that one, too. Limberti told me it had first been made in 1956 and later rendered immortal in a snapshot taken of Queen Sophie of Spain and the Princess of Liège walking down Via Condotti in Rome carrying Gucci 606 and Gucci 607 handbags. One had a top clasp with the two overlapping sides whilst the other had a big G with a central closure.

Both items were styled by Limberti, even though one design probably originated from my grandfather Aldo, who had called Limberti from New York instructing him to fashion exactly that type of purse – one with a clasp on top instead of on the front.

Visiting my father at the Gucci laboratory felt rather like being on a carousel of wonderful things to see. I was agog with curiosity.

One day a few years later, I was going to Via delle Caldaie after school. I went into the warehouse on the ground floor and followed Ezio, the storekeeper, who was about to pull out a bolt of beige cloth printed with diamonds. I helped him carry it upstairs to the leather goods department. There, Ezio unrolled the cloth on the table and after a few hours was fashioning a suitcase. It had an iron frame bordered with brown leather or brindle-patterned pigskin. It was truly lovely. Ezio started working with the glue, then the well-marked seams, the red and green ribbon on the exterior, and of course the inner lining. The suitcase had spacious inner compartments, with a distinctive elasticised crimped edge.

My father came in. A little fearfully I said, "Father, I'm here." "Oh," he said and looked very carefully at the fabric, then remarked, "These two diamond shapes that meet right here, let's try to put the two Gs there." It looked just right – the two Gs met impeccably in the corners of the diamonds. Then Rodolfo, Aldo's brother, also popped in, followed by Vasco, who was often there. They talked it over and finally agreed on the idea. Endless trials, meetings and discussions followed on how exactly to position or join up the two Gs – closer up or further away, one overlapping the other or one upright and the other upside down. At last, they came to a decision. And that is how the celebrated interlinked GG trademark was born. It comes as no coincidence, given that those letters were my great grandfather Guccio Gucci's initials.

The event marked not only the birth of the historic Gucci trademark but also my great excitement at seeing the origin of such an important symbol. It was no longer a mere design. Thanks to the interlinked Gs, our family would go down in history. To our endless wonder, those two simple initials turned out to be a huge success.

My Uncle Rodolfo had lived in Milan for many years, adopting the Milanese style that distinguished him from his brothers. He dressed meticulously, with his tartan jackets – quite showy at times – looking very good on him. This was thanks to the elegant demeaner he had acquired from his years as a movie actor.

Rodolfo prized all that was beautiful and admired stylish people. But he was a self-centred man. When he called somebody at the processing workshop or in the shop, he would not give his name but merely state, "Hello, it's me," as though the person on the other end should know automatically who he was.

Of the three brothers, Rodolfo was surely the one who – thanks to his savoir-faire – excelled in customer relations. He was the perfect PR man, while contributing less to the business and design sides of our operation. He doted on his son Maurizio and lived in the memory of his wife Alessandra, who had died young. However, being so self-absorbed, Rodolfo's attention towards his son was limited mostly to financial matters. It was Grandfather Aldo who became an important teacher for Maurizio.

As time went on, my father, as the volcano of new ideas that he was, began thinking about how to plasticise textiles. His ideas were always challenged by his father, uncles and brothers. But he was stubborn and determined, so doggedly pursued his pioneering vision.

He contacted the Firestone Company in the US but the experimental tests were disappointing. Then he tried with Italian companies, and again met with failure. Not happy, he even turned to Germany and this time, his efforts paid off. Yet this development, too, proved short-lasting because my father wanted to use Italian materials.

Then, he finally pulled it off. Gucci started a line using plastic-coated fabrics, at first with diamond-shaped patterns only then later, in 1968, with the interlinked Gs. The line was produced in several colours including beige, blue and red.

The Americans responded enthusiastically. Right behind them, came the Japanese, where the Gucci licensee for Japan was the well-known Mr Motoyama.

In those same years, the search for alternative products reached fever point. However, the notion of making men's shoes first came to us in the 1950s. That was the heyday of loafers, with the original version of these shoes without laces hailing from the Anglo-Saxon world. It was a brilliant concept yet even more brilliant was the notion of placing a horse clamp on the top of the shoe. The horse theme was our distinctive feature in earlier years and we continued this concept in a myriad of ways. This line of fine loafers sewn by hand in the traditional manner became hugely popular. My father managed to find an excellent traditional craftsman for the job. The initial productions were stunning, even though the leather was a little stiff. In the later series, the leather was treated to be especially soft and supple. Thereafter, a red and green ribbon was added under the clasp and, finally, a red and green gilded enamelled badge.

The shoes were exported to the United States. Between 1968 and 1970, on average 300 pairs sold each day. This celebrated slip-on was called the 175.

Then came the 1266 handbag with the stiff cornelian handle. followed by the 1235, a rectangular purse with a shoulder strap in gilded metal chain.

My father loved designing new accessories, such as the Gucci wallets with a jockey's cap in coloured gilded enamel.

In 1965 came jewellery and watches. The company produced wrist watches with a gold strap and a semiprecious stone dial in lapis lazuli or tiger's eye. I still have one of the latter and vividly remember the man who assembled the watches and created the dials as being a highly skilled and warm person – Mr Renzo Vanni from Impruneta, near Florence.

The year 1966 saw the production of the rectangular-shaped wallet with a quaint half-opened, gilded hand. Delightful. The hand-shaped clip closed the wallet at the back, over the compartment for paper money. Many thousands were sold over the years.

The flooding of Florence's Arno River on 2nd November 1966 proved to be a tragic and terrible event. I was twelve years old then and in shock.

As soon as we learned that the river was breaking its banks and would likely submerge entire neighbourhoods, I went to the window and in utter bewilderment saw the floodwaters approaching. Amid the general uproar, I sat on the steps at the front door with my poodle Topsy on my lap, absolutely terrified. I watched the water come in the door and flood the cellar. Night had fallen, people were shouting and climbing on the roofs crying out for help.

Heedless of the fright and general commotion, our nanny Pina was busy collecting the basic necessities we had decided to bring with us. My mother tried to reach my father by phone but the lines were down. He had stayed on at the Via della Vigna Nuova shop at the other end of town to salvage what he could from the incoming sludge and ended up getting stuck there for the whole night and part of the following day.

That night, the boiler also exploded, letting out a sickening stench of diesel oil. My mother, Pina, my sister and I were all ready to escape on an amphibious vehicle supplied by the fire brigade.

Fortunately, this proved unnecessary as the water stopped rising two steps short of the level of the bedrooms and sitting room. But the entire ground floor, the billiard room, the playroom and Pina's bedroom were completely submerged.

When my father reached us the following day, we ran to him and burst into tears of relief.

Meanwhile, the floodwaters had subsided, leaving only mud behind. Our house, the garden and the street presented an awful sight. It was truly upsetting.

My sister and I spent a few days in Bagazzano, at Uncle Roberto's country house in the hills near Florence. The property belonged to his wife Drusilla Caffarelli. Then, we were packed off for three months to Rome to stay at Nanna Olwen's while my parents worked hard in Florence to get the house, shop and production facility back on track. The following year, in 1967, a new Gucci shop opened on Via Tornabuoni.

At that time, grandfather Aldo was in the US, managing the first Gucci shop in New York. As it was difficult to find groceries for some time in Florence, he would send us tinned meat. It was called Simmenthal, then a relatively new product in Italy.

I wanted to be an archaeologist

At the end of the 1960s, I left my peaceful and happy childhood world behind for the stormy years of adolescence. I felt uncertainty and a need to make my own decisions. Now was the time for me to build an identity of my very own.

The happiest memories dating from that time are from the long holidays I took with my parents.

Every period of my father's life was defined by his sudden consuming passions which, more often than not, petered out due to his volatile character. Just before that happened was the time for trips and snapshots.

My father loved discovering special, exotic or untouched places, while my mother and we children followed quietly and obediently behind, carried along by his uncontrollable energy. Our first destination was Kenya, in East Africa. My father fell in love with Africa and we went back several times. The next destinations were Tanzania, Uganda, the island of Lamu, then again Kenya on the trail of the white elephant, and finally the Ivory Coast. My sister Elisabetta, my mother and I made up the miniature caravan that followed behind my father and his many cameras. Of the many bags he carried with him, two bulged with telephotos, film and lenses.

In Kenya, we travelled in minibuses. After long hours clattering over uneven and pot-holed roads, we would reach our destination dog tired and dazed. We always headed for national parks where we stayed in comfortable lodges and slept on camp beds. At night, it was not a question of shutting the door but of zipping up your tent. In the dark we heard sounds coming from the savannah and lions growling in the distance. The next morning, we woke at dawn to a classic cup of "milk tea".

One day, after a difficult journey on bad roads, we reached Lake Rudolf (now Lake Turkana) in the Rift Valley, on the border with Ethiopia. The place was extraordinarily beautiful with its remote and inviolate lake so vast you could not see across to the other side. Flamingos inhabited the banks. When they flew off together, they looked like pink clouds crossing the sky. The lake was famous for its abundance of fish, especially perch.

On our arrival, a man who spoke perfect English came out to greet us. His name was George and he was the proprietor of the lodge. Although born in London, he had been living in this remote locality for years. George wore shorts, a white vest and no socks, in the African manner. But I was surprised to see him also wearing beautiful Gucci loafers, the ones with the red and green stripe and the clamp on the buckle – the famous 175 Gucci loafers now on display in the Metropolitan Museum in New York. My father also noticed it and asked George where he had bought them. He answered that they were a gift from a rich client who loved this place and often spent his vacations here.

Our next destination was Tanzania, the Serengeti national park and the valley of Ngorongoro. Given the distances, we flew from place to place in small planes. One morning, we took a five-seat Piper to fly over the mountains and enjoy a bird's eye view of those incredible panoramas. As we were waiting to board, the pilot arrived. We noticed how young he looked. Rather puzzled, my father asked him: "How old are you, anyway?" The pilot answered proudly: "I'm nineteen!" My father turned to us with a weak smile and a meaningful look: "Quite a young fellow. Let's hope for the best!"

On those trips, we laughed a lot. My father was always able to bring out the innate Gucci sense of humour – that light ironic touch he himself never lost, not even in the most difficult of times.

As I was then struggling with my own misconceptions and a strong need for attention, I often did not grasp this side of my father's character. I felt something breaking inside. My typical adolescent restlessness prevented me from getting the best out of those wonderful places, my parents' company, and all the other good things. Incredible though it seems to me now, I did not consider myself a happy person.

When I was fourteen, I started at the SS. Annunziata boarding school at Poggio Imperiale. So, now I was a 'Poggiolina'! SS. Annunziata, where I was specialising in modern languages, was known for its glamorous pupils, from Maria Jose of Savoia to actress and model Marisa Berenson. Now the darling nuns of my childhood school were a thing of the past. Here the so-called Signorine, as our instructors were called, were strict and damn sadistic. Inside the school, we wore a uniform – a grey smock with a light blue sash around the waist – and a hat and cloak when we went out. I was then beginning to rebel against authority, whether at school or at home. Feeling quite ridiculous, I refused to wear the uniform. I was rude to the teachers, burst into tears when I was given bad marks, and often got low marks in conduct. Yet I managed to pass every year.

At home, I could not bear getting scolded. "Don't do this, don't look at that." Thankfully, a consuming passion had just then taken hold of me: drawing. I had lessons from a teacher who came from the Porta Romana Art School, a well-known institution in Florence. I spent long, blissful hours painting and drawing – two things I was good at. Throughout those same years, I also took a course in designing clothes and even earned a diploma for it.

I saw little of my father and missed him. He was always away and rarely spent any time with me. During the Christmas holidays, he was adamant that I work at the new Gucci shop on Via Tornabuoni, which was then doing extremely well. I actually enjoyed being there and learned lots of new things. When I got home, I was expected to give a detailed account of the day's events at the shop – which items were most in demand, which were selling well. My task was preparing parcels, assisted by the shop manager.

It was clear to me even then how important and coveted Gucci products were. Once, five or six young boys came into the shop. One of them, the most enterprising of the group, shyly asked for a silver keychain. He paid it with all the change he had in his pocket, which he must have been saving up for months. The boys left the shop proudly, overjoyed with their buy.

I worked under the watchful eye of Uncle Roberto, the shop manager. Roberto expected all staff to observe a certain dress code. The women wore a skirt, which in his opinion were more elegant than slacks. We also had to have a smile on our faces and be extremely polite with customers at all times.

At the beginning of the 1970s, during a vacation in Sardinia, I met Stefano, my future husband (and future ex-husband!). I had just turned seventeen. Stefano was an architecture student and always carried a copy of Rinascita magazine with him. I was struck by his handsome looks and blue eyes. Stefano was not part of Florentine society, in fact, he came from Perugia. By chance, I learned that he was studying at Florence university. When my vacation was over, I left him my telephone number. Some time elapsed without hearing from Stefano. One day, as the summer of the following year was approaching, the phone rang and to my great surprise, I recognised his voice. My heart started beating fast. This is how our friendship began. That summer, he invited me for a camping holiday on the island of Lipari. It was a new experience for me and I couldn't make up my mind whether I was more excited or more apprehensive at the prospect. We left Florence – me with my usual hard-sided suitcase, he with a tent large enough to accommodate two people comfortably. Once in Lipari, we headed for the white-sanded beach. With all his good intentions, Stefano took hours pitching our tent. As I sat on my 100-kilo suitcase and watched him work away, I sank further and further into the sand. It was evening when he finally finished. We crept inside the tent. That night, a powerful wind blew the tent down and we slept under the open sky. It was a wonderful holiday. It was so much fun and I still fondly remember it to this day. The days went by and I fell more and more in love with Stefano. As he came from a simple family, my parents took a rather dim view of the whole affair, which did lead to some problems.

Although my boyfriend and I were quite different, his intellectual side strongly attracted me. I was now reading more books and meeting his university friends.

This encouraged me to take a new path in life. I wanted to continue my education by studying archaeology at university (and Stefano was probably pushing for this). I chafed at the thought of having to fall in line with my parents' expectation that I work for the family company. The rule in Casa Gucci was that as soon as you became an adult, you went to work for the company, just like my grandfather and my father had done. Starting from the bottom would help us learn all aspects of the business.

My father, too, had started working in the Gucci shop in Rome when he was barely out of high school. It often happened that grandfather Aldo would call Olwen at 8:00 in the morning, telling her to get my father out of bed and send him down to the shop. Later on, my father was sent to Florence to work full time at the Gucci shop there. My father wanted us to do the same. Thus, my strong passion for archaeology led to some conflicts.

My parents were beginning to have their first serious arguments and for this reason, too, the atmosphere at home was tense. Tired of Italy, my father wanted to go and live abroad. His business commitments and trips, as well as the Gucci laboratory in Scandicci near Florence, which he had been chosen to manage, were claiming more and more of his time. Our company now counted nearly 200 employees.

On my eighteenth birthday, my father gave me a second-hand Fiat 126. I found a lovely Gucci leather handbag inside the car. It was brown, oval-shaped and with a rigid handle – almost too ladylike and grown-up for me, but I was overjoyed nonetheless.

Having my own automobile gave me the freedom I had long craved. Now, I could go to Siena to attend my archaeology classes without having to take the bus.

With my new car, I had the whole world at my feet, even though I travelled at a snail's pace, given my inexperience behind the wheel. Here I was, an adult and free to make my own decisions.

On the way to Siena, I stopped wherever fancy took me, even just to buy a sandwich. Other times, I would give a friend a lift and we would chat happily all the way. Still today, the Florence-Siena highway is wonderfully scenic as it cuts through the beautiful hilly countryside.

Having reached Siena and parked my trusty little car, I would walk over to the university. It was a big, ancient building. In the early days, some students looked at me condescendingly, given the age-old rivalry between Siena and Florence. "What is a Florentine doing here?" I never gave heed to their snide comments. I was there to study and that's all that mattered to me.

Classes were small, averaging about ten students. This made it easier for us to get to know each other. Classes at Florence university, in contrast, were always overcrowded.

We got onto a familiar footing with our professors right from the start. When classes were over, we would go out in a group and have lunch at a small trattoria nearby. Many subjects came up but mainly we discussed a projected dig at Villa Settefinestre. This was a totally new experience for us.

Professors Andrea Carandini and Daniele Manacorda insisted we all call each other by our first names, which helped us develop a good relationship with them as well. The small number of students also allowed the professors to monitor our studies more closely.

I drove to Siena almost daily. A classmate often rode back with me to Florence so we could prepare for exams together. It was wonderful to study the ancients. The university organised trips to archaeological sites in Tuscany or Paestum or Ostia Antica. Our guide, Carlo Pavolini, was a well-known archaeologist.

After successfully passing the initial exams, I grew even more passionate about archaeology. It was thrilling to study a subject I had personally chosen. Recognising that I had so much intellectual curiosity was also a new experience. The discovery of landscapes and places that had been inhabited by other peoples in remote times only added to that excitement.

Freedom is something not acquired by blunt force but by savouring it little by little with steadfastness and determination.

I was entirely happy with my choice of studies. One of my professors, Andrea Carandini, was a renowned archaeologist who had studied with Ranuccio Bianchi Bandinelli, author of an important book, Archeologia e Cultura Materiale, published in 1975. The book was the first to stress the importance of students' active participation in archaeological excavations.

So. this is what I did. In the summer, we excavated at Villa Settefinestre, on the Aurelian Way near Orbetello. The villa dates back to the time of the Roman empire. Armed with our picks and chisels, we drew ever nearer to the Roman layer. It was pure excitement. A group of us students spent nearly three months on the job alternating between courses, digs and conferences. We slept on cots in a building owned by the Orbetello municipality. The alarm clock went off at 6:00 in the morning then we would head off to excavate until lunchtime, when the heat forced us to stop. I took part in the Settefinestre dig for three consecutive years. How wonderful it was to discover the ancient Roman villa! Mosaics, frescoes and thousands of objects like amphorae, coins and necklaces materialising out of the soil. We took turns at the different tasks. One of us brushed dirt off a mosaic, while another carefully scraped the brittle areas with a spatula. I was even nominated "Miss Excavation"! That was one of the great periods of my life.

Naturally, nobody in my family supported my archaeological studies.

Whenever my father came back from the US or England, he always greeted me somewhat hastily. Right after, he would surprise me with an unexpected question: "How many exams have you taken?" I would answer, "Not too many, to tell the truth but I am still busy with the digs." To which he invariably concluded, "If you left your studies, you could come to the laboratory and start working there. That way, you would learn to do something useful."

His words set me on edge and I didn't know what to answer. He was such a distant father but every time he made a suggestion, I would take him seriously and try to follow it. I felt that every wish he expressed confirmed my claim to his affection. He did exert a powerful influence on me.

At last, I decided on a course of action that would satisfy both of us: mornings at the university, afternoons at Gucci. However, reconciling work and school was complicated. Thus, slowly and reluctantly, I left my studies with a promise to myself that I would take them up again later.

But in the end, I permanently abandoned my plans for a university degree and went to work full-time for the family business. My social life continued with salons and gala dinners. With Stefano, who was now competing in tennis tournaments, I made new friends. These included Tommaso Montesi Righetti, the Frescobaldi family, and Guido Martelli who owned a lovely mansion.

Three very lively boys

Grandfather Aldo's children – the third generation of Guccis – were three very lively, fair-haired, blue-eyed boys. Giorgio was the eldest, then came my father Paolo, and finally Roberto, whose mother Olwen had nicknamed him Sunny.

Giorgio, the only survivor of the three, now lives in Rome. Thanks to his strong sense of humour, he hides any anxiety and faces problems with a light-hearted quip. Like my father, he has always loved horses and the sea, and has a definite aesthetic sense. As a young boy, he was the sweetest of the three – a patient, caring, highly sensitive person. Alas, as the years passed, his patience wore thin and his warmth took on a tinge of harshness. Giorgio got on well with my father; they were very similar. In spite of the conflicts that arose within the family business, Giorgio proved to be the closest to my father. I think he really loved him.

As a young man, my father Paolo had a thick head of hair which he lost by the time he was thirty. From the earliest years he was the most restless and enterprising of the three brothers. His mother's favourite, he loved her back in equal measure.

Roberto, the youngest, was tall, thin, with long hair and the bearing of an English gentleman. People said he looked like David Niven. Often it was hard to understand what he had on his mind, as he always seemed so detached from everything. Roberto had great savoir-faire, behaving tactfully and formally with everybody, He dressed with sophistication, wearing only custom-made shirts with high, round collars fastened with a gold pin. He died in October 2009, leaving behind his wife Drusilla and six children.

The one trait all three brothers shared was a strictness in raising their offspring. They did not bother with compliments or displays of affection. Nor did they promote their children's careers. To the contrary, they kept the spotlight on themselves as sole players in the show. This trait they probably inherited from the family patriarch, the formidable Guccio Gucci – and from their father Aldo, whom they addressed with the formal "Voi" (the custom at that time).

When Elisabetta and I were children, we spent lots of time with our cousins – Giorgio and Roberto's children. We were all about the same age and would meet at Uncle Roberto's country place in Bagazzano, near Florence, and at the seaside in Versilia. And of course, also at Nanna Olwen's home with the garden and swimming pool in Monte Mario in Rome. Afternoon tea always included a delicious and very English plum pudding.

Elisabetta and I have always been very different people. As children and teenagers, we had more in common but as we grew up, we developed two really distinct characters.

Over time, out life choices diverged. At eighteen, I started actively pursuing higher education, yearning to set myself apart from my family background. Elisabetta wanted to raise a family. I always tried to fulfil my dreams, expectations and wishes, at times ignoring the demands of everyday life. My sister was practical, down to earth and made children her priority. We are two very different people, and have consequently lived different lives, yet always try to keep in touch.

As the years passed, we somewhat lost touch with our cousins. When my father was at loggerheads with his family, the cousins strongly criticised me and sided with their respective elders. Unlike them, I dealt with these issues from my own point of view, knowing I must follow my own path, defend myself and not yield to psychological pressure. Although this decision caused me some suffering, my determination and wish to achieve success in my career not only protected and sustained me but helped me avoid getting overly involved in family squabbles.

I do not believe children should pay for their elders' mistakes. Today, when we cousins meet up, a new feeling of kinship unites us. We know that we belong to a great family and that we all had difficult relationships with our fathers.

Like his brothers, my father also started working from an early age at the Gucci store in Rome.

Later, he was sent to Florence to manage the production site in Via delle Caldaie.

Roberto ran the Florence store. He, too, had a bold sense of humour – one of the distinctive characteristics of the Gucci men – and was wont to dispense wry witticisms. Given his talent in public relations, he built up excellent contacts with our foreign clients, creating an import-export and franchising network that promoted the Gucci trademark worldwide.

My father used to tell me that when he and his brothers were children, they were always up to some sort of mischief. Keeping them in line was a real problem. A string of nannies came to look after them but soon got scared away by the pranks they devised to test their resistance. The only one that lasted for a good number of years was Esterina, a tall and energetic woman. My father often spoken of her.

Paolo, Giorgio and Roberto took great delight in thinking up the most bizarre tricks to try their nannies' patience.

My father remembered how on more than one occasion, they put a pail of water above the door to Esterina's room, leaving the door ajar. Then they created some pretext for her to go to her room – to fetch them a pullover they had left there, for example. Unsuspecting, she would enter her room and get a pail of water dumped on her head.

Another episode involved Emma, yet another nanny. After dark, the boys lined up all their shoes along the hallway that led to their room. In the middle of the night, they started shouting for Emma, complaining of a terrible stomach ache. She rushed down the hallway, tripping and falling all over the shoes as the boys laughed their heads off in their room.

The brothers also had plenty of quarrels among themselves and sometimes little Roberto even had to climb up a tree to avoid getting knocked about by the other two.

The family always had their beloved dogs. With them, the three boys came up with a great pastime: racing in the garden. Paolo would fasten Rongo, the Great Dane, to a small cart he had found in the garage of their Roman house. Then it was Giorgio's turn with his cocker spaniel, and finally came Roberto with his black poodle. The dogs would run like mad. Naturally, Paolo always won. Only once was he bested by Giorgio and his cocker spaniel.

As they grew older, all three brothers found they were strongly attracted to and charismatic with women. As teenagers, they discovered that from a loft in the house, they could see through a window into a nearby gym where some pretty signorine were working out. This was so exciting that apparently one of the brothers once nearly fell out of the loft.

During the difficult time of the mid-1980s, when my father wanted to leave the family business and create a line of his own, he discovered that his brother Giorgio was the only one willing to speak with him in depth. Eventually, however, even Giorgio found it hard to listen to my father. He would not pick up the phone or answer at the door. "Signor Giorgio is in a meeting," "Signor Giorgio just stepped out." Not being able to get his brother on the phone, one day my father hit on a brilliant idea.

After calling Giorgio for the umpteenth time, my father called his secretary, "Hello, Roberta, the fire department has just called to say that my brother's house at Porto Santo Stefano is on fire.

I must speak to him immediately!" That time he did get through. Of course, there was no fire.

When my father passed away, I tried to find a second father in both his brothers. This proved impossible due to their stand-offish nature and I eventually resigned myself to the overwhelming loss.

My great-grandfather, Guccio
Gucci, founder of the company.

Below: The document from
the Chamber of Commerce
attesting to the opening
of the business (1923).

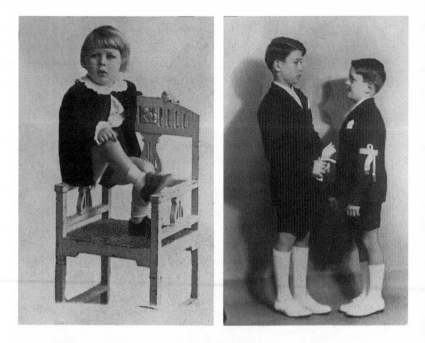

Left: my father Paolo. Right: his brothers Roberto and Giorgio as young boys.

My father Paolo at the age of 17 years.

My mother Yvonne at the age of 18 years.

In Forte dei Marmi with my sister Elisabetta and my mother Yvonne in the 1960s.

My mother Yvonne and my Nanna Olwen on our boat, the Ennovy.

My Nanna Olwen with all of us grandchildren lined up on the stairs one Christmas Eve.

Us cousins at the house on Via della Camilluccia in Rome.

Uncle Vasco, my grandfather's brother.

My grandfather Aldo Gucci
with my sister Elisabetta.

My father Paolo with my grandfather Aldo.

My mother Yvonne with a guest at the inauguration of the Gucci shop on Via Tornabuoni in Rome, 1967.

Below: Me, my mother Yvonne, my sister Elisabetta and my cousin Maurizio at an event for the film by Rodolfo Gucci, *Il cinema nella mia vita*, at the Odeon Cinema in Florence, November 1971.

Queen Consort of Greece, Federica di Hannover, and her daughters, Sofia, later Queen
Sofia of Spain (left) and Princess Irene of Greece and Denmark, in the 1960s.

My grandfather Aldo Gucci with Kim Novak.

My uncle Giorgio and Audrey Hepburn, 1963.

My father Paolo and my
Nonno Aldo at the first
parade in the shop on Via
Condotti, Rome, in the 1970s.

A model parades a fur coat in fox.

Me with my grandfather Aldo, Vittorio Gassman and his wife, Diletta D'Andrea, at the inauguration of the shop in Rome.

Below: With my cousin Marizio.

My grandfather Aldo Gucci.

My uncle Roberto Gucci.

Uncle Rodolfo Gucci, my
grandfather's brother.

My father Paolo in the 1990s.

It all started at the Savoy Hotel

The Gucci family business started long ago, in the early years of the 1900s. Those were very different times from today. Having never experienced those events, I can only reconstruct them from the stories I heard from my elders.

My great grandfather Guccio Gucci, the man who created the trademark that bears his name and became a hallmark of Italian creativity the world over, was born in Florence in 1881 to Gabriello Gucci and Elena Santini. Documents surviving today take our family line back to San Miniato al Tedesco, where a Palazzo Gucci still exists. The Guccis had noble origins and the city authorities always granted their descendants important posts and honours. The archives include a family tree and even the family coat of arms.

Guccio's father, Gabriello, worked in a hat factory in Signa near Florence. Signa excelled in the weaving and crafting of straw for hats. Florence, too, was renowned for its arts and crafts, which at that time constituted one of the city's most important resources. When Guccio's factory ran into trouble and business experienced a downturn, the young man began to dream of a different and brighter future. He wanted to leave home and go travelling, like so many young boys in all eras.

His curiosity and enterprising spirit took him to England. At that time, Florence was already a destination of choice for many foreigners, especially for the English, who came flocking to the city to admire its art treasures and surroundings. What's more, the newspapers in those days were full of tempting stories about London, then one of the capitals most favoured by both European and American high society.

So it was that in 1898, Guccio – a determined and enterprising young man – sailed to England with just a few pennies in his pocket. He was barely seventeen. When he arrived in London, he went to the Savoy Hotel and boldly asked to be employed there as a doorman. Built in 1889 and situated on the Strand, a few steps away from Trafalgar Square, the Savoy was at that time the swankiest hotel in town and known the world over.

Guccio was quite good looking. He was thin, not too tall and dressed in a sober and distinguished manner. His only weakness was sporting frivolous vests. Accordingly, he reported to the manager wearing his precious vest. The man was favourably impressed by the young Italian. Guccio was hired as a liftman inside the hotel – lifts being quite a new thing at that time. Opening and closing lift doors all day was a humble and tiring job. But overjoyed with his new environment, Guccio never tired, treasuring whatever experience came his way. On his days off and in the evenings after work, he even found the time to study. Ambition spurred him to learn perfect English, German and French, regularly using them at work. Thanks to great enthusiasm and a desire to discover this fascinating new world, Guccio took careful note of every detail and profited enormously from the new environment. The lobby always bustled with important guests and famous people from all over the world, carrying of all sorts of luggage. The entrance was piled high with suitcases, leather bags, hatboxes and shiny leather trunks studded with metal hinges and buckles. Guccio was especially taken by the initials and monograms of their owners. This rendered those objects all the more exclusive. Seeing this, he recalled the workshops back in Florence that specialised in crafted leather goods.

Some four years later, the lure of the Tuscan countryside and the sweet smell of his homeland beckoned. Guccio, proud of having earned some money and gained experience, went back home.

A year after returning to Florence, in 1902, Guccio married Aida Calvelli. She worked as a helper in her father's tailor shop. Aida was gifted with a strong character, lots of energy and a nose for business. They produced five children: Ugo, one girl named Grimalda, Enzo (who died young), Aldo, Vasco and Rodolfo. Aida was extremely frugal, even saving bits of string which could be used later on.

After serving in the Italian army during the First world war, Guccio went to Milan. He quickly found employment in the Botto leather goods workshop, then went on to work in one of the shops of the well-known Ditta Franzi. Ditta Franzi had been established in the mid-19th century and also specialised in leather ware. Guccio soon became the Managing Director there.

At Franzi's, my great grandfather learned a lot about processing and selling leather products. In spite of his many business trips, he longed for his home town and often came back to Florence. One day in 1922, while he was strolling in downtown Florence with his wife, he spotted a vacant shop on Via del Parione. The idea flashed into his mind that this was the ideal place for him to realise his dream of opening a leather goods store in his home town, selling travel bags and purses painstakingly crafted but reasonably priced. The shop he saw on that street seemed perfect and his dream soon became a reality.

In 1923, Guccio Gucci went to Chamber of Commerce in Florence and registered his new shop on Via del Parione 11 with the name: "Valigeria e Articoli da Viaggio".

In those days, the name Gucci was not featured on the shop sign. Nobody considered putting the surname on the products either, as this did not seem necessary. Guccio started buying tanned hide and leather from Germany and later on from the celebrated English tanneries. From England, he also brought back the idea of using horses and horse-lore as themes in crafting ornamental details on his goods: horse saddles, saddlebags, bridles and travelling trunks. The famous red and green ribbon came a little later. Conceived as an ideal decoration for bags and suitcases, it was nothing more than the horse's saddle-girth, skilfully crafted and assembled. In 1932, Guccio opened a second shop on the more important and central Via della Vigna 7. The enterprise then moved to Via della Vigna 11.

A few years down the line, in 1937, Guccio also opened a small workshop on Lungarno Guicciardini, in the heart of the city. There, for the first time, the sign read "G. Gucci".

There was a lot of work to be done. The business now needed skilled craftsmen to meet the wishes of a growing clientèle. When the Lungarno Guicciardini workshop got underway, it had only eleven workers. Many buyers were simply passing tourists. But Italian and foreign aristocratic families from the Rothschilds to the Frescobaldis – and the solid Florentine middle class as well – visited the Gucci shop to purchase the luggage they needed for travelling.

In 1944, Florence was bombed and the workshop suffered extensive damage. Vasco would roam the city looking for pieces of marble or wood to do repair work on the shop, which in any case swiftly became known for its high-quality crafted goods. In those days, it had become common for people to travel with custom-made luggage personalised with their initials. Guccio met all their requirements. He was very clever when it came to dealing with his clients. One of the most sophisticated items he produced was a small-sized leather travelling bag, similar to a beauty case, equipped with a row of small silver-capped bottles in repoussé crystal, a powder compact, hair brush and comb (also in silver). The owner's monogram was stamped on the case. Then came the garment bag, deemed a must for a sophisticated lifestyle.

In those days, a shop owed its fame and importance to satisfied clients who spoke of it in high terms. Advertising, as we know it, didn't really exist. Guccio was very good at his work. The key to a prosperous business consisted in the quality and careful finish of the goods. And it was these two elements that spelled this plucky Florentine craftsman's success. But Guccio's skill consisted also in selecting qualified labour. He was a polite and extremely meticulous person who communicated the passion and love he had for his work to customers and everyone else.

In 1946, Umberto of Savoia, nicknamed the May King due to his brief rule, managed to name Guccio Gucci "Purveyor to the Royal House of Italy". Later on, the Italian Republic bestowed on my great grandfather the title of "Grande Ufficiale del Lavoro". Many types of suitcases, trunks, travelling cases and handbags were ordered directly by the clients and personalised as per their requirements, with figures stamped in gold and inner compartments. Guccio invented a family crest based on the family coat of arms, with a horseman holding a suitcase in either hand, a rose in one corner, and the wheel of fortune in the other. This symbol came to be referred to as the "Gucci Crest" and was later used on handbags or embossed on the zipper pull. The Gucci shop endured as a destination for important clients, from the international jet set to famous actors, princes and queens, who never imagined such an elegant place could exist.

Passion and poise

As the shop grew, so did Guccio's children. They still used the formal "voi" form to address their father which certainly created some distance between them. Yet, their decisions would prove crucial for the future of the family company.

Guccio had been a strict and determined parent as well as a brilliant entrepreneur and his children honoured his legacy. First and foremost was Aldo, the apple of his father's eye. By now, to own a Gucci item or to give one as a gift had become a real sign of elegance and good taste.

Uncle Ugo was a tall, stout, broad-shouldered man. I don't remember him very well since he was the eldest of Guccio's offspring and passed away when I was still a child. But I do remember his son Giancarlo, a kind man who worked very hard. He specialised in the metal accessories used in Gucci products.

Of Guccio's sons, Vasco was the one who most closely resembled his father physically. He, too, was very creative and put all his talent into developing new products which soon became all the rage. Vasco loved to hunt and, as probably the most social of the brothers, would host massive dinners for his friends in Polcanto, near Florence, where he had a fine house and a game preserve. He loved being out in the countryside, spending Sundays with friends and returning to the shop on Mondays.

But he also often went on trips, seeking out ideas in France, in England, where he would visit all the markets and shops in search of objects or "trinkets" that he could then remake in leather.

Vasco created a series of gift items themed on hunting and horses. I remember a chess set and lovely drinking glasses with silver-embossed animal heads – deer, hare, wild boar. The objects were soon in great demand. Vasco also designed objects for picnics, such as horn-handled cutlery. Or a pen holder shaped like a gun case. Then there were animal heads to decorate leather items. Another item that proved highly successful was a desk set produced in crocodile skin. Then came the hand-stitched golf bags crafted in leather. These items were almost exclusively manufactured by Gucci at that time.

Vasco had a good heart, as one would say. Being a unique spirit with good taste, he was the peacemaker between the brothers Aldo and Rodolfo. He wanted them to have a good relationship. Even with his brother Rodolfo, Aldo would try to take over any decisions, not allowing the others to have any say. This would leave Rodolfo often feeling somewhat resentful, not least because Aldo was always very successful in everything he did.

Having been a heavy cigar and pipe smoker, Vasco died in 1975 in Florence after suffering from lung cancer. Knowing that his days were numbered, he had himself taken to a hotel instead of a hospital, checking into the Grand Hotel "Villa Cora", which in those days was truly splendid. Perhaps nearing death there would make it seem more like heading off on a holiday for one last voyage.

Not having had any children, Vasco's transfer of his stake in the company was pivotal. The Gucci corporate bylaws stipulated that the shares had to pass to the male members of the family only, along with management of the company, hence his share passed to Aldo and Rodolfo, who both held 50%.

Aldo passed on 10% of his own shares to his three sons in equal stakes, making them shareholders for the first time. Hence came the third generation: Giorgio, Paolo and Roberto.

Rodolfo, however, had only one son – Maurizio – who was also third generation but, as already explained, was much younger than his cousins so he did not yet have any shares. Perhaps Rodolfo didn't think it was the right time to give him any, as he was still so young. After all, Maurizio would receive his shares after his father's death.

Rodolfo, as the youngest of the three brothers, was the only one who had spent some time working in a field unrelated to the family business. He, too, was quite attractive, with a captivating smile. As mentioned, he managed to have an acting career that began when he was in Rifredi, near Florence, where the company S.A.C.I.A. – at that time a production company – had set up to shoot some scenes. My uncle offered up his services to the director, who immediately accepted.

Shortly after, Rodolfo found himself in Rome. It was 1931 and Rodolfo was just seventeen. The film director Mario Camerini noticed him and offered him a minor role in one of his films. Camerini then chose Rodolfo to be lead actor in the film "Rotaie". Cast alongside Rodolfo, working under the stage name of Maurizio d'Ancora, was Kate Von Nagy, already somewhat famous and a very pretty actress. This role ended up opening up the movie industry to my uncle.

It was Camerini who thought up the stage name of Maurizio D'Ancona, also motivated by the fact that Rodolfo's father Guccio did not approve of his son becoming an actor and so asked him to use a pseudonym.

Film was silent at that time but this particular production ended up being dubbed in four languages.

When the war broke out, the Cinecittà Studios went through a rough time and Rodolfo found himself without work. He had already met his wife by this time, so the family business was his only option for work and to earn a living. For Rodolfo, it was no easy choice. He wanted to continue acting. His wife Alessandra – who had a very strong and decisive character – was pushing him towards going to work for his father, Guccio. Ultimately, it was decided that he would go to Milan, where a shop was eventually opened.

So whilst Rodolfo's time in the film industry did not last long, he did manage to became a popular actor. My uncle acted in thirty films, alongside such famous actors and actresses as Valentina Cortese, Vittorio de Sica and Emma Gramatica. He also worked with Anna Magnani, notably in the 1942 picture "Finalmente Soli". Magnani became a dear friend of his, often visiting the Gucci store in Rome, which was inaugurated in 1938.

On set, he even met his future wife, the actress Sandra Ravel, whose real name was Alessandra Winkelhauser.

Aldo's wife – my Nanna Olwen – and Alessandra soon became good friends. Both foreigners, with Olwen being from England and Alessandra from Germany, they would meet in Rome during the German occupation and often go out to spend time together.

As to Uncle Vasco, I recall him in his office at the Gucci shop on Via della Vigna Nuova. He'd be comfortably ensconced in his big brown leather armchair, surrounded by photos and hunting trophies. Like great grandfather Guccio, Vasco smoked cigars and spent lots of time at the shop.

One day, a telephone call informed us that Queen Elizabeth was planning a visit to the Gucci store. It was 1961.

The place was all in a dither and was polished until it shone. The female shop assistants were dressed in grey suits, floral decorations hung from the walls, the visitor's book lay open for signatures. The commotion was such that on the appointed day, the street filled with curious onlookers, while photographers rushed to the scene, cameras flashing. Soon the crowd in front of the store was enormous. The only person missing was Her Majesty the Queen, who had meanwhile cancelled her visit due to the pandemonium. We were greatly disappointed.

Vasco was a kindly and generous person. He always cared for his employees, who he treated like family. He would even give them an advance so they could purchase a house when they needed.

Aldo, too, loved his employees. One day at the Casellina establishment, he noticed that one of his workers was upset. "What is the matter?" he asked. Giuliano answered: "Mr Aldo, I broke the spectacles I've been wearing for years and I can't afford to buy a new pair." Aldo told the man to follow him upstairs to his office. In his presence, he called an optometrist and ordered new glasses for him.

As regards Vasco's devotion to his work, I was informed about a humorous conversation that took place between him and Mariarosa, who worked at the cash desk. It took place late in the evening when the shop was closing for the day.

"So, Mariarosa, how much did we make today?"

"About four million, eight-hundred thousand lira, sir" (which quite a high sum for those days).

"Really? We absolutely must reach five million!"

"Sir, it's seven in the evening, how can we possibly?"

Stroking his chin, Uncle said: "I'll tell you how. I'll buy a wallet right now!"

Rodolfo and Sandra went on to have a child, Maurizio, named after his father's stage name. Unfortunately, Sandra died only a few years later, in 1954, when Maurizio just a little boy.

During part of World War II, Rodolfo was stationed in Rome as a military attaché in the film section of the General Staff. He received official permission to continue acting and moved to Venice during the time that the Italian Social Republic was trying to set up a new film studio, similar to Cinecittà, at the Lido. After the war, the Italian film industry got back on its feet. But Rodolfo went to work for the family company instead, having being pressured both by his father Guccio and his wife Sandra, who was a practical and resolute woman. Concerned about his son's future, in 1949 Guccio opened a store in Milan and appointed Rodolfo as the manager.

Grimalda, Guccio and Aida's only daughter, sat behind the cash desk in the Gucci store in Florence. This post demanded a great sense of responsibility. It wasn't easy for a woman to work in those times. Aunt Grimalda was an elegant lady, with fluffy, back-combed blond hair. She often invited me to her house to spend the afternoon with her (rather boring afternoons, to be honest) and enjoy tea and cakes. The moment I would rise to leave, my aunt would immediately plump up the cushions, wipe away any bits of sugar and put the tea cups back on the tea tray. She was a wise and well-balanced woman. She married Giovanni Vitali, a Florentine, but had no children.

My grandfather Aldo was a lovely and most charming man, and the dynamo of the three brothers. Guccio relied very much on him. Aldo was always on the go, itching to get every new Gucci initiative underway.

He met his wife, Olwen Price, in the Gucci store in Florence. She was a refined, shy English girl, with a sweet manner and enchanting blue eyes. It was love at first sight. Perhaps it was that English charm of hers that won him over. They were married in 1927.

Grandfather Aldo talked incessantly about business, his projects and his success in the United States. I clearly recall the time he came back from New York and extracted from his pocket a lovely little bottle with a thin strip of red and green enamel set in the glass, bearing a brown and gold cornelian cap with the initials GG. This was the prototype for the future Gucci perfume bottle.

Aldo would ask us grandchildren to choose the perfume we liked the most.

Yet my memories of him are not always pleasant and sometimes leave a bitter taste in my mouth. My grandfather did not get on with my father – theirs was a love-hate relationship that produced endless conflicts. Whenever I happened to be within earshot, Aldo would beat his fist on the table and with an angry voice exclaim: "Ah, that father of yours! He doesn't understand a thing! He always wants to do things his own way and never listens to me!" I would get frightened and start crying, not comprehending why I should be the target of his bursts of anger.

When great grandfather Guccio saw that his restless son Aldo wanted to expand the family business, he agreed to have a Gucci shop opened in Rome. That was in 1938 and Aldo went happily off to the capital. The location was Via Condotti, in downtown Rome, where celebrities such as Audrey Hepburn, Sophia Loren and John Wayne would stroll by in later years.

During the war, it became difficult to find premium materials. The Gucci brothers devised ways of developing simpler means for crafting their goods. First of all, they utilised wicker along with wood and bamboo for the handles. The latter idea in particular came from the fact that Uncle Vasco collected walking sticks and one of these was bamboo. After the war, fabrics such as linen and jute were added, paired with small pieces of leather. We also produced wicker baskets and stiff raffia bags.

In the post-war years, the four Gucci stores – two in Florence, one in Rome and one in Milan – were doing well. The secret of their success and popularity was that the Guccis personally oversaw them. The three brothers curated every aspect of the business and knew well how to pamper their clientèle. They also had a knack for choosing the right business associates, managers and employees.

Aldo, the most enterprising brother, would walk down Via Condotti and go into the classiest stores seeking top-notch staff. When he found someone, he first looked them up and down carefully, then with his customary cheek asked point blank: "What is your salary here?" Somewhat intimidated and knowing who he was, they would answer, "100,000 lira." He would respond, "Come to work for us and I'll pay you 200,000." And, of course, they would agree.

All our shop assistants greatly admired and respected the Gucci brothers, even though they knew them as exacting bosses. The staff had to be neatly dressed at all times, be smiling and ready to meet all client requests.

It was almost a Gucci ritual to organise Sunday lunch for all of the shop assistants and workshop employees, who would attend with their families.

In the Florence shop, there was a sort of piggy bank. If Uncle Vasco found too much dust on the display tables, the shop assistant responsible for dusting would have to pay a fine, which would be dropped into the piggy bank. The money was then donated to the Madonnina del Grappa charity institution.

Being thrifty and avoiding any waste played an integral part in the Gucci family tradition.

Throughout the 1950s–60s, Gucci stores were frequented especially in Rome and Milan by glamorous customers: Alain and Natalie Delon, the Duke and Duchess of Windsor, Kim Novak, Clark Gable, Paola of Liège, Grace of Monaco, and so many others. Whenever celebrities showed up (particularly at the Rome shop), paparazzi and photographers regularly gathered outside. On such occasions, the special clients were ushered into a private room and were often honoured with a small Gucci gift item, such as a foulard or a belt. Nelson Rockefeller came into the shop one day and said to my Uncle Giorgio, "I admire what you have managed to accomplish in the United States. People who come all the way from Canada to buy Gucci moccasins in your Fifth Avenue store."

When I was working on the historical archive of the Gucci company, I discovered an anecdote concerning Princess Grace of Monaco and the birth of the Flora foulard.

One day, the princess entered our shop in Milan looking for a flower-patterned scarf. At that time, however, all Gucci scarves were themed around hunting and horses. Store manager Rodolfo did not flinch – he promised the princess he would have one crafted exactly as she wished. He instructed the costume designer Vittorio Accornero de Testa – a man he had met during his movie days and who now worked for Gucci – to design a foulard with a floral motif. Drawing inspiration from Botticelli's Spring, Vittorio traced a cascade of intense, colourful flowers. The foulard counted thirty-six tones – truly a record-breaker given that each had to be printed separately.

At that time, not even Hermès produced their famous scarves yet. Our Flora turned out to be a huge success, so much so that the same pattern was later used to make blouses and silk dresses.

Anecdotes abound relating to famous people who were absolutely devoted to the Gucci brand throughout those golden years. For example, the great Totò would visit the Gucci shop in Rome and, while looking at the wares, would ask for "a nice cup of coffee" to be brought to him from the celebrated Café Greco on Via Condotti. Rossano Brazzi always showed up at 7:30 pm, just as the shop was closing, and would then go with Grandfather Aldo to the kosher restaurant Da Giggetto to feast on Jewish-style artichokes.

One fine day in the 1960s, Great Garbo came into our Florence store. Tall, dressed in black and hiding behind sun glasses, she tried to go unnoticed but the girl at the cash desk recognised her right away and called Uncle Vasco, who came rushing down from his office to welcome her and help her make her purchases. In the end, Garbo bought a solid black handbag.

Irene of Greece was another devoted client. She would come in, always looking elegant and understated, and select an item. Before leaving, she would pass the cash desk, stroke Mariarosa's cheek and say, "How are you, my dear? Now, don't forget to send the bill to my home." It goes without saying that Uncle Vasco never did.

Rodolfo oversaw our store in Milan. Owing to his cinematic experience, he was truly adept at flattering the ladies. He would kiss their hand with a flourish and pay them lavish compliments, thanking them warmly for having visited the premises. They would inevitably make their purchases then off they would go with a beautifully wrapped Gucci item.

Aldo in Rome behaved much the same way. He would painstakingly describe to a prospective customer how a handbag was made, how it would match a certain coat or suit. He would take the handbag and strut about with it, almost always managing to sell not only the handbag but also some other accessory along with it.

New York, New York!

In the 1950s, the Gucci business was flourishing. My grandfather, Aldo Gucci, was sure that the time had come for our family business to expand abroad – to the U.S. in particular. After discussing the matter over at length with his father Guccio, who did not see eye-to-eye with him on this very ambitious project (he thought America was too far away), Aldo left undaunted for New York. In this particular enterprise, he proved how farsighted his vision could be. He was convinced that the Gucci business, having totally won over the Italian market, would meet equal success everywhere else and that New York – given America's immense economic potential – would provide the ideal launching pad to spread the Gucci trademark worldwide.

On his own initiative, Aldo set off for New York together with Rodolfo to explore the city and test the project's feasibility. He found a space that seemed suitable on a side street off Fifth Avenue. He was then joined by Vasco, who was also convinced that his brother was on to a good thing. In spite of the favourable beginnings, Guccio continued to be pessimistic about the venture. He was afraid the whole thing might ruin their many years of hard work. He would confide to one of his associates or employees, "Did you hear? Aldo and Rodolfo want to go to New York. I trust Aldo – he always has his head on his shoulders. But Rodolfo?"

The two returned to Florence but Aldo went straight back to New York. The year was 1953. A little while later, he opened a store on 7 East 58th Street.

Aldo very skilfully built up his success in America, capitalising on the ability of Gucci products to combine the great tradition of Florentine quality crafts with Italian savoir faire. A blend of graciousness and class.

In an interview with The New York Times in 1980, Aldo rather poetically said that he was "taking Florence's Michelangelo to America and was proud of taking Florence's historical treasure to the world."

The uniqueness of Gucci products arose from a sense of the majesty of Florentine art, its birth amid a wealth of beauty, its dazzling aesthetic. The Guccis were like that, too – sophisticated, elegant, passionate. They had an instinctive eye for both beauty and things well-crafted.

Yet, success did not come right away. The war had left its mark and the first significant items made by Gucci were based on simple materials. In 1955, we exported handbags made of a type of fabric called 'tripolino', or 'Leonardo' – a type of jute with motifs of flowers, small pineapples or a series of knots. In the 1960s, textiles with diamond shapes were imported, as well as the GG plastic-coated fabric, along with the brindle leather handbags and suitcases.

Aldo travelled to Florence often, bringing lots of photos with him which he then showed to the modeller, saying, "Look, these are the bags women have in the States, let's keep them in mind." The American bags thus inspired new models. This processing step took time. The design on paper came first, followed by the cardboard model. This model was then positioned on the finer board – a somewhat stiff, unwoven textile – to create a model in real size, which could be studied in the event that alterations were needed. Once this model was ready, a fresh cardboard model was made and placed on top of the leather that was then cut to the same shape. Finally, the parts were glued on and everything was stitched together.

Aldo made important friends amongst the international actresses in Rome, thanks to his brother Rodolfo's former acting career. The

Gucci store in New York was set up very well, from the interior to the display of the goods, to the salespersons. At the entrance was a striking white-gloved porter, just like in our Italian shops.

Aldo's charisma and strong personality won over the Americans. My grandfather attended many social events, where he met significant people who added glamour to the Gucci brand. Jacqueline Kennedy became a regular Gucci customer. The "J.", a famous cross-body handbag, was named for her. Following the success in New York, which showed that Aldo's expansionist instinct was correct, Gucci shops opened in London and then Paris.

Back in Florence from the U.S., Aldo called Vasco and pulled out a photo from his briefcase. "See this? It's me with Richard Nixon. I'm starting to become famous!"

We also credit Grandfather Aldo with having devised a motto that sums up the company philosophy: "Quality is remembered long after the price is forgotten." This phrase, stamped in gold on leather, was framed and hung in a conspicuous place in every Gucci shop. In 1961 or 1962, Aldo called Vasco's secretary from New York and said, "I'm sending you something special in an envelope." A short time after, the enveloped reached the office. It contained a cheque signed by "John Fitzgerald Kennedy". The President of the United States had purchased two suitcases and three handbags.

The check was later framed and hung on the wall in the office.

Of Aldo's three sons, Giorgio ran our Rome store, Roberto the Florence store while, also in Florence, my father Paolo managed our worldwide franchising network, the creative work, production, and the workshop. The workshop was the real engine of our business. In 1971, it was relocated to Scandicci outside Florence – in a hamlet called Casellina to be precise. My father had overseen every detail of its design and construction.

In the U.S., meanwhile, the New York store was soon followed by more stores in Palm Beach, Beverly Hills and Chicago. Grandfather Aldo would come back to Rome or Florence and gather all of us – children, nephews and nieces – around him to narrate his American achievements. We listened to him, overjoyed and thrilled. Great-grandfather Guccio never made it to see his business prosper to its full extent. In 1953, at age 72, he died of a heart attack in his home in Florence, on Via della Farina, where I later spent my childhood.

Gucci had become much more than a simple trademark or a leading enterprise in its field. Its products represented a true status symbol, a sign of class, distinction, luxury and good taste. Over the years, the production diversified. In addition to handbags and luggage, we started making accessories: belts, foulards, perfumes, lamps, ashtrays and prized watches. My father Paolo especially valued the latter. He was the one who conceptualised the famous ceramic animals – the leopard and the cheetah. And the enchanting heads of horses that had earlier been made in wood by the renowned Florentine craftsmen Fiorenzo Bartolozzi and Giuseppe Maioli, being later made in ceramic ware by the Scandicci supplier, Paolo Marioni.

When I first started working in the business, I often had to go see a craftsman in Impruneta, just outside Florence. An unassuming individual, no longer young, he skilfully engraved watch dials by hand. He studded the dial with wonderful semi-precious stones – lapis lazuli, tiger eye and malachite. Then, he inserted the gold minute and second hands and completed his handiwork by hooking on the stiff gold bracelet. It was wonderful to watch him work.

Clothing also became a crucial item in our production. In the 1970s, "Gucci fashion" burst on the scene, although in the previous decade my father had the Via delle Caldaie factory manufacture the first leather skirts with fur trim. Indeed, my father, with the invaluable help of my mother and the modeller Signora Martelli, had invented the first leather underskirts. He instructed Roberto Meciani, one of our designers, to paint small butterflies on the leather. Neither Uncle Rodolfo nor Grandfather Aldo liked the idea. They hinted, "Well, those butterflies are a bit ..." My father pushed his point and said: "Okay, put them in the shop window and if they don't sell, you can bring them back to me."

Following those early experiments, my mother found a softer material with which to make leather clothing, a nappa that was produced by a glove manufacturer, who had been producing gloves that had a watch attached. The garments proved to be a true success and sales were excellent. Another hit was the blouse made of three scarves using the famous Flora pattern. Competition in those days daunted none of us – Gucci products had no peer. Hermès was the only competitor Aldo did fear, with simultaneous admiration. He would make believe he didn't know of the French fashion house but when he pronounced the name, he would say, "What's the name of those stinkers, I mean the ones whose name begins with an 'H'?"

My father, rather, was somewhat obsessed by Hermès handbags, which he said were especially soft. He bought an expensive one in leather and took it downstairs to the modellers' workshop to have it disassembled. Between the outer leather and lining of Hermès bags was a layer of nappa – an extremely velvety kind of leather. This was why Hermès bags were soft.

Seeing the disassembly made me want to die – how could he take apart such a beautiful handbag? In those years, Ferragamo was producing shoes and perhaps also starting to make handbags. But our catchphrase was always: "What's that one starting with an 'H'?"

In the 1960s and 70s in the Unites States, Grandfather Aldo went from success to success thanks to his skill in public relations and sales management. During an official meeting, President Kennedy shook his hand and said, "You are the most important ambassador of the Italian style."

Frank Sinatra, Ava Gardner and a host of other Hollywood actors – the very heart of American cinema – were clients of ours. In Woody Allen's picture Manhattan, we see shots of the Gucci shopfronts to evoke Fifth Avenue's posh atmosphere.

Not to be outdone, Cadillac – the famous American carmaker – started producing a limited series of 1979 Seville models with an exclusively-designed Gucci interior. The leather seats were striped with the red and green motif, whilst the interlinked GG logo was embossed in silver on the dashboard. In the boot was a full collection of Gucci suitcases and travelling gear.

It was around this time that an order arrived from London: Prince Charles requested a set of crocodile suitcases – perhaps intended as a gift for his mother, Queen Elizabeth II.

All throughout this period, there were many inaugurations – in Manila, Seoul, Taipei in Taiwan, Stockholm, Barcelona, Marbella, Athens, Aruba in the Netherlands Antilles and in Monte Carlo, where the evening continued with the Rose Ball, where we would present everyone with a Flora scarf, being dedicated to Princess Grace.

Usually, I went alone or with the marketing manager. My relatives did not go as they had delegated me as the representative of the family and the company. This was no easy task.

Tokyo and Hong Kong had also been clamouring to open Gucci stores. I remember reading in a 1983 issue of the Italian weekly magazine L'Espresso. In an interview with Italy's then-President, Sandro Pertini, during his prosperous trip to Japan, he said: "When I went to Osaka, two Japanese ladies sang a song ... two elegant and beautiful women sat down beside me ... they immediately exclaimed 'Gucci, Gucci', showing me their pocketbooks, cigarette cases, evening handbags and shoes, saying they were made by Gucci. I got the impression that for the Japanese, Gucci is like a God!"

One day, a distinguished gentleman from Tokyo walked into our store in Florence. His request to buy more than one hundred handbags sent the staff into mayhem. For him, money was no object – he simply wanted to have these famous bags at any cost (he was obviously going to resell them back home).

The most important event at that time was the inauguration in June 1980 of the latest Gucci store in New York, also located on Fifth Avenue.

The shop had been remodelled by architect Ernest Castro and occupied four levels reached by a glass lift that offered visitors a view of the entire store. The flooring was in travertine, a precious Italian stone, whilst bronze statues beautified the spaces.

The ground level featured displays of handbags and accessories on beige carpeting. The first level was devoted to menswear and leather goods. The women's section was on the second floor. Here, stunning evening dresses and fur coats stood out gloriously against the ecru-coloured background. Finally, the top level housed the famous "Gucci Gallery", designed by Giulio Savio, a major Italian architect of the latter half of the last century.

The furnishings were incredibly luxurious. There were Renaissance tapestries on the walls along with impressive art works by internationally-known artists such as Giorgio de Chirico, Amedeo Modigliani and Roy Lichtenstein. The Gucci Gallery concentrated on jewellery and the most valuable items, including the handbags with the interlinked shoulder straps in gold chain.

This area was reserved to Gucci clients of the highest standing – those seeking the most exclusive items. It was skilfully managed by Signora Lina Rossellini, wife of Renzo, the brother of the famous film director Roberto Rossellini. With her class and refinement, she could put any "special clients" at ease whenever they were in search for the necessary calm required to select the most exclusive gifts. For a select elite, Grandfather Aldo had conceived a golden key that allowed them to directly open the door onto this magic world of luxury.

Our New York store was not only patronised by the Kennedy family on a regular basis but also by Ronald and Nancy Reagan as well. Our most devoted customers additionally included Peter Sellers, Richard Burton, Liz Taylor, Maria Callas, Mr Revlon and Mel Brooks. Indeed, Brooks rendered us an unforgettable tribute in a scene from his 1974 picture Blazing Saddles where the sheriff rides a magnificent black horse on whose saddle the Gucci trademark is clearly shown!

When my grandfather is evoked through my memories, anecdotes and photos, Aldo Gucci appears in my mind's eye at his desk, smoking a pipe, his eyes bright at the joyful thought of having conceived such a wonderful and unique place.

Working in the family business

When I decided to drop out of university and go to work for the family business, I suspected it was going to be difficult – not physically, of course, but psychologically, given the intractable character all Guccis had, including my father. He and I both had the same strong and determined nature which often made for the sharp arguments that are typical of two people who admire but also fear each other.

In the morning, I would get up bright and early to be at the office by 8:30. Initially, my job was simply to keep the office papers in order. Very soon, I spoke up and, trusting in my drawing abilities, asked to be assigned to the creative department. I didn't get what I wanted just like that. Indeed, it was quite complicated to even reach my father, as I had to go through his terrible and snappy secretaries first. My father was always busy and uneasy yet in spite of this, I continued to deeply admire his talent and his pioneering ideas.

But sometimes, he gratified me. He would burst into my studio and, taking me affectionately by the hand, announce that we were going to visit the production factory. This is how I got to know all the workers personally, from the man who assembled the handbags to the warehouse foreman to the gilder working on the buckles (the gold had to be strictly 3 microns) along with the staff in the creative department. My father had all the designs for new projects hung up on a line, like photographs drying. He would study them for some time, circle around them, look at them in perspective, then point with his finger, "That one!"

Well, clever people do have rather unusual ways sometimes!

When my father went to the factory, you could immediately sense his mood. Even the way he coughed and dressed could be telling – if he took off his jacket and put on his burgundy sweater, it signalled that his mood was upbeat. If he kept his jacket on, you could expect a black day. In that case, a warning would be passed around for everyone to be on alert.

He would walk into his office, sit down and look at his desk. It was always piled high, messy and overflowing with an endless array of all kinds of small objects that he would collect: bits of leather, discarded samples, semi-precious stones that could be used either on the bags or clothing, along with random sketches. Newspaper clippings bore photos of handbags, drawings and roughs. This is where the mind created the objects that have gone down in history. Then there was the hardware, with clasps, snaffle bits, snap hooks, hinges, rings, small chains, a heap of metal accessories and even a little set of metal horse bits that could also be used as inserts on shoes.

The scraps of leather in particular were a great source of strength. He would put them in the drawer then maybe even a year would pass before he would take them out and say, "This is what I was looking for!" before going on to create the colour or type of leather for a future collection of bags or garments.

It was truly the desk of creations. And amidst that chaos, my father was able to find everything.

Indeed, it was from here that many of his ideas and inspiration came so woe betide anyone who dared try to put things in order!

Yet, my father could find inspiration anywhere. Peering out the window one day, he saw a van full of all sorts of wicker baskets. Remembering the items that his grandfather Gucci, his father Aldo and his uncles had made during the war using leather and simple materials, he immediately called the concierge to find out who that van full of baskets was for and to have the supplier come to his office. This is how a purse shaped like a small trunk was born. It was fastened at the top with a little leather flap.

Thus came another idea of a basket bag in brindle leather, open on two sides and clearly designed to be taken to a beach in St Tropez.

The interlinked Gs were also of his conception, designed as a gilded metal accessory on many types of studs and clasps to snap the bags shut. That time, too, despite his brilliant intuitions, the rest of the family opposed him.

My father used the Tuscan word 'ciappina' to refer to the leather reinforcement that secures the handle or shoulder strap to the handbag. He adopted marine snap hooks as fasteners for handbags and put lots of big and small pockets inside to lend the item a practical and original touch. He often added a shoulder strap to the bags, as a necessary touch of practicality for the bag whilst the boat carabiners then became a must for the clasp on the most beautiful bags. All of these were fruit of his ability to invent.

Whenever Grandfather Aldo would visit Florence from New York, there were lots of arguments and disagreements. My grandfather caused my father no end of frustration. Sometimes my father grew so furious that the moment Grandfather left to go back, he would go down to the shipping department and – purely out of spite – stop all deliveries to America. Some days later, the warehouse foreman would come to ask, "Mr Gucci, when are we to send the packages to New York?" My father would pro-crastinate for some days until he had sufficiently cooled down before telling the man to go ahead.

My father was also a business man who knew how to look after his factory, often going to the workers' area, even checking the bathrooms to see if any workers were hanging out in there longer than they should have, perhaps to smoke. Indeed, he would quite regularly find people hanging out there and, often in quite a harsh tone, would tell them that their break was over and to get back to work.

My father always wanted to distinguish himself but with his own father, he just couldn't manage. It was a constant challenge. Aldo's character dominated over everyone.

The relationship between my father and my grandfather was fraught from the start, given their strong and similar characters. Every idea my father would come up with, my grandfather refused point blank, often without even listening properly. When Aldo was in Florence to talk about his many achievements in the U.S., he would cut a smart figure in his double-breasted jacket with a flower in the buttonhole as he passed around photos of the celebrities he had met, almost as though he were asking for commendation and applause.

Yes, Grandfather criticised and scuppered my father's proposals all along the way. Whilst my father considered innovation crucial and a sign of a healthy creative spirit, Daddy never missed an opportunity to dampen his son's enthusiasm.

Discovering new trends and ideas in selecting both products and materials was a passion for my father. Almost all the other family members – including Rodolfo – wanted to stick to the tested lines of Gucci leather goods and handbags.

A kind of rivalry was also evident when father and son met for the two-yearly meetings to pinpoint the Autumn-Winter and Spring-Summer collections. My grandfather, who didn't like others making suggestions, only wanted to showcase his own ideas and would shut my father up by ringing a bell. Invariably, my father countered with an acrimonious, "Okay, Daddy."

One day, my father found a catalogue on his desk of an exhibition of paintings by one of our workers. He was so impressed by it that a short time later, he asked the man to design a scarf. This soon became the famous Gucci Tiger foulard. Other designs followed and Roberto Meciani became one of our company's chief designers. He was the one who designed the doves and the mushrooms.

Paolo Gucci was usually strict and somewhat abrupt with the staff. To be forgiven for his verbal extremes, he would send them flowers.

To this day Maria, one of his employees, recalls an occasion that characterises my father's manner. It was the afternoon when Maria went into his office and timidly asked for time off the following day as she had a dentist's appointment. After a moment's silence, my father cleared his throat and asked, "So, which tooth hurts, Maria?" Maria blushed. She didn't really have a dentist's appointment and had come to realise that it was not so easy to pull the wool over Signor Paolo's eyes.

When I was at the Gucci production plant, I used to enjoy nosing around in the orders department. Frank Sinatra had ordered a desk set in green, silver-studded crocodile skin. A wealthy American lady who lived in Beverly Hills had requested a pair of sandals with solid gold chain straps. Ava Gardner was a compulsory Gucci handbag collector and had more than a hundred items. Even Jacqueline Kennedy had ordered a black crocodile skin bag with a clasp in real gold. The likes of Gianni Agnelli, a devoted client of ours, one day ordered some crazy amount of photo frames with his initials on them to give to his grandchildren.

Meanwhile, I was getting better and better at my job. I was now in a section of the creative department that specialised in jewellery and objects.

On some occasions, my father would even ask me what I thought of the new models for handbags.

Although I was reasonably satisfied, sometimes I also felt neglected as my name was never on the list for upcoming meetings or programmes. I convinced myself to be patient and went on with my work, waiting for a more important role in the family business.

When I sometimes did try to interest my father in an idea of mine, he would brush it off. The one time I pressed him with a report, he grew so angry that he took my papers and threw them down the stairs, shouting that I must be patient and not always try to have things my way. That was very humiliating.

Casellina

T he factory in Casellina was built by architect Enzo Ciar-
detti, with the help of chartered surveyor Giovanni Vitali,
who was the husband of Grimalda Gucci, Aldo's sister.
Right after the 1966 flood in Florence, new construction projects
started outside the city centre. The Gucci family bought land in
Casellina/Scandicci and established a leather goods production
hub there that was to become world famous.

It was a modern, dark-beige marble and glass building facing
Autostrada A1. Later called "Gucci 1", this factory was inaugurated in 1970–71.

As the new factory was coming about, my father had some
great ideas (like a football field for the workers).

The factory was surrounded by a large and very striking
garden with a green lawn that my father, a passionate gardener, had filled with rare plants, including Florentine iris and
Tuscan cypresses. True to the English half of his blood, my
father created a lake that was full of water lilies and various
breeds of duck, including the mandarin duck. There was even,
if I remember correctly, a lovely white swan along with two
peacocks.

Paolo even wanted to add a swimming pool for the workers to
use in their free time and told my grandfather about it. Known
for his common sense, my grandfather immediately made fun
of him, quipping, "So, then, what are you going to do? Become
a lifeguard?"

There were lots of jokes among the staff as well, including during the lunch break when one employee could not resist asking, "Roast duck today?"

The building was of a very high standard and had elegantly furnished offices. 200 employees worked in four departments: modelling, cut-outs, prototypes and production. The giant hall with its huge windows bustled with activity as buyers were met and samples were put on display.

This later became the venue for fashion shows.

The factory's upper level accommodated the fifty-plus employees who worked in the sales and distribution department, along with the designers in separate quarters.

My father had given the offices something of an American flavour, based on the open-space concept, with glass partitions only. This was meant to suggest a perfect team spirit amongst the workers. My father's office was at the centre – from there, he could see everything.

Paolo, my father, was at the helm of all this. He came to the office every day and was the one who gave the designers their instructions, would feel and purchase the leather for the models, and had the vision to conceive highly-innovative business strategies. He always made sure that his team was hard at work.

Given that lunch was provided to the workers, my father had created a model dining hall, engaging Chef Ezio Burbassi, who had worked for many years in Florence's Ristorante Il Campidoglio. My father ate with his employees and used the lunch break to listen to their problems, their joys and their ideas.

Travellers passing by on the highway noticed the imposing Gucci building and thought it was some luxury hotel. They were not far off the mark, for it was here that luxury and the authentic "Made in Italy" style came into being.

In addition to all this, the long and straight avenue that led to the factory was where I learned to drive. Just short of my eighteenth birthday, it was my greatest wish – the wish all young people have. And it was my father who took on the daunting task of teaching me.

At that time, he owned a light-green Citroën Mehari. This was the vehicle we used for the lessons. But the gearshift was close to the wheel and also higher than in other cars, which caused me some difficulties at first. Straight, rather long and without much traffic, the road stretching from Scandicci to the front door of our factory was an ideal road for learning.

Still, driving lessons were torture for me. As usual, my father was a strict and rather testy instructor. I had to do exactly as he said, manoeuvring this really cool but damned difficult car. After countless trials and errors, I did learn – and very well, too. But what a task!

The Casellina factory turned out products that became truly iconic. We started manufacturing new types of handbags made in different types of leather, such as ostrich and baby crocodile.

My father developed a Summer-Winter line. For summer, there were items based on symbols like anchors featured on scarves and beach bags, abat-jours with a compass, and purses of course. Men's ties bore designs of anchors and ropes. Production was going full steam ahead.

Each department – footwear, handbags, luxury goods and jewellery – had its own designers. The scarves turned out to be so lovely and innovative that people framed them like paintings and decorated their homes with them. My father was the prime mover of all this – he controlled all activities at the plant, with every item passing through his hands and subjected to his scrutiny. He said that all Gucci stores must sell the same merchandise. Uniformity in the decor, style and standard applied to the newly-opened stores as well.

Those were not easy times for him, as he had to push his ideas which the others often disagreed with.

In 1985, my cousin Maurizio decided he wanted to make Gucci sneakers. My father loved the idea and immediately had samples made – white sneakers with a red-and-green stripe on one side only.

However, Maurizio, with his ideas of grandeur, suggested: "Let's get Adriano Panatta to do the publicity." The tennis champion responded enthusiastically but asked for sky-high payment.

This led to a lively debate. Aldo said, "Think of all that money! Besides which, we don't need to pay anyone to promote our wares." My father sat upright in his chair and said, "Exactly!" But Maurizio insisted so much that they all got into a heated argument.

Ultimately, Panatta was dropped but the shoes were made anyway.

It was at this time that the clothing stage went into high gear. What had until that point in time been hand-crafted goods grew into an important business.

Various fabrics were used for the clothing range but, naturally, leather was the material of choice since it represented our brand. Indeed, leather was used for trousers, vests and jackets, with other materials being fur (an important textile) from guanaco, zebra, leopard and other skins, as well as GG-marked textiles for the weatherproof wear.

My father, who was passionate about the clothing line, himself wore GG leather trousers and jackets.

The fashion shows, expressly organised for international buyers, were held directly on the premises. These were real parades. I remember how awed I was when the stunning Paola Dominguin, daughter of Lucia Bosè, once appeared on the catwalk.

On the day of the fashion show, nobody dared utter a single word inside the factory. My father would nervously pace back and forth, making sure that everything was just right, with all the models dressed according to plan and all the garments perfectly paired. He really wanted his work to be acknowledged and appreciated by his public, not only the clientèle. For him, it was not just a matter of pure and simple production – each collection was, if I may put it such, like a "child" of his being born.

In the 1970s, an invigorating gust was blowing through the Gucci business. There was great anticipation ahead of the first fashion show that was to be held in our Via Condotti store in Rome.

Prominent people had been invited, along with journalists and important Gucci clients. As the days went by, preparations reached fever pitch. Everything had to be just so, from the individual garments to the matching accessories, to the models wearing them.

My role on this occasion was to be an attentive and curious onlooker. It was an unforgettable experience to see the garments I had heard my parents discussing over lunch or dinner at home now paraded in front of my eyes.

This was the first official Gucci fashion show that was not held at the production factory. On the day itself, I was overwhelmed with excitement. It wasn't only the items on show but the models who seemed to have stepped out of some glamour magazine. A display of luxury, elegance and class. I stayed behind the scenes with my mother (who had had a direct hand in organising the show) and enjoyed the pageantry.

Being there filled me with pride. It gave me joy to see my family in such harmony with itself. And I also experienced a sense of awe – there they were, not satisfied with mere congratulations but also listening carefully to people's critical evaluation.

Grandfather Aldo, who had initially opposed the clothing line, was also ecstatic. He rose to his feet to thank all the guests with his usual pleasantries then added, "I would also like to thank my son Paolo for all his work, and for the success of this line."

I was happy that my father had reached his goal at last.

Grandfather Aldo, my father, Uncle Rodolfo, Roberto, Giorgio, and a still-youthful Maurizio were all present for the event. This was perhaps one of the last times I would see the Guccis assembled together and looking truly satisfied. Afterwards, they all went to Café Greco to toast their success with a glass of champagne.

To my mind, their fashion concept was unique – nobody else was doing anything like it.

The fur coats, the capes, the zebra overcoats, the silk blouses with the snaffle-bit design (only later were they produced in the Flora print) ... all had extraordinary class.

Another major fashion show – the first and last of its kind – was held in the White Room of Florence's Palazzo Pitti, then a much sought-after venue for such events.

Significant orders kept coming from the U.S. Indeed, Nancy Reagan ordered a special handbag for her appointment as First Lady at the White House, whilst actress Joan Collins ordered an evening bag in green lizard skin with a gold chain shoulder strap.

Gucci was a family matter. Everybody had their own opinion, which often created tension.

Every so often, everyone would huddle in the boardroom: Grandfather Aldo, his brother Rodolfo, my father and his brothers. They would be in there for hours, arguing and discussing animatedly, with Aldo's voice always heard clearly above the others. Terrified, the staff and I always stayed away. Then suddenly they would all come out, looking relaxed and smiling.

When I met him in the hall, Grandfather Aldo would express his satisfaction that I was working for the business and contributing to its success. "For every grandchild, a new shop!" he was fond of repeating. His brother Rodolfo, too, also often made the rounds of the Gucci factory, loudly declaring: "I am the CEO!" He was a unique character but he did not get on with my father. In a reproachful manner, he would call me "Paolina" – little Paolo – identifying me by my father.

Like my father, Rodolfo also loved creating new handbags, thus fostering a competitive climate.

On one occasion, he added a model of his own creation into the samples. There had already been disputes, and when my father saw the bag, he took it and threw it out the window. The following day, the gardener found it and brought it in, saying to my father, "Signor Gucci, I found this bag in the garden. Do you know anything about it?"

Then, as fate would have it, I went back to work in the marketing office on Via delle Caldaie. In those days, Gucci staff worked in a huge frescoed room. After being renovated in 1975, it was used as an office space. Stefano, who was now an architect, restored the frescoes. My father gave him the job and I was happy he had chosen my fiancé over other candidates, thus showing his regard for him.

One of my tasks in that big room was to organise dinners for the buyers who would come to Florence twice a year to view our collections. I took great care in decorating the table – every evening there was a different theme and I would call the soloists from the local Music Academy to come and play for us.

One particularly successful evening, as I remember, I had invited a theatre company from Venice to stage the Arlecchino. Each actor was presented with a gilded, red-and-green striped Venetian mask. Nonno Aldo himself, while we were seated at the table, rose to his feet and said, "Congratulations, Patrizia!" I was overjoyed – his accolades were so few and far between!

But there came a time when the tensions between brothers and sons boiled over. Passionately wanting his family to acknowledge him as artistic director of the Gucci Company, my father came up with the idea of opening a separate office that would serve as a container for his artistic and creative projects for Gucci merchandise.

There was no way. Not one of them, including his father Aldo, supported it. That was a difficult time.

But at last, my father opened his own workshop in Florence, asking my sister and me, together with a designer and a modeller, to join him. Proud to work with my father, I resigned from the family business.

The new workshop turned out to be a powerhouse of creativity, creating handbags, purses, suitcases galore!

My father's imagination was daunting. Yet his relatives gave him no peace. On a daily basis, he received threatening telephone calls, especially from Rodolfo. But the more they tried to thwart my father, the more he forged ahead.

He wanted only to develop a line of his own – the Paolo Gucci line. But the project never took off because he was prevented by law from using the family name for his own creations.

After this, it was really difficult to be around my father. After a number of bitter clashes, I returned to the family business – a better environment, I thought, for finding my own fulfilment. Once back at Gucci, I picked up where I had left off. It wasn't easy and if I did fit back in, it was thanks to Maurizio's benevolence. It was he who was at the company's helm throughout those years, the 1980s.

Returning after some two years away, it was quite a difficult environment. My father had left, leaving behind lots of conflict and confusion. Inevitably, I was left to shoulder the repercussions. I had become the scapegoat. It was truly a humiliating period.

I was asked to wear the Gucci uniform and given a desk somewhere in the corner. My job was to type up business letters from dictation, something I had never done before. They were unkind, sometimes not even calling me Signora Gucci but only Patrizia, and even monitored my telephone calls.

I got a time card to clock in and out of work and if I was a few minutes late, an hour's pay was detracted from my salary. Having perhaps received instructions to treat me like any other employee, I was not allowed to read any corporate documents or notices and was even harassed on occasion.

Eventually, I was instructed to work as a buyer but even in this role, I was carefully observed. Time and again, I vainly rebelled against having to wear a uniform – the objective was merely to deprive me of my identity.

My days at work seemed endless. But I held on, fought tooth and nail, and slowly managed to fit in again. This was also thanks to my excellent rapport with Maurizio, which was based on a sense of mutual admiration and respect.

At last, I was given a decent assignment. I became head of Gucci's international PR and travelled a lot, taking the family image around the world. Throughout those years, I opened more than thirteen stores in different countries, from Spain to South Korea, to the Philippines.

There was even an inauguration party for the Montecarlo store, with the festivities that evening continuing with a Rose Ballet. For the occasion, the ladies were presented with a Flora-patterned foulard – the same one we had created for Princess Grace of Monaco.

At last, thanks to my dedication and persistence, I managed to acquire a role of my own inside the family company. This was truly gratifying for me. I was now acknowledged as a true Gucci, one who spoke in public, gave interviews and established contacts with international agents. Powered by my enthusiasm, I oversaw things down to the last detail and achieved excellent results. I was now the Gucci World Ambassador.

One business trip involved a visit to Manila. Arriving after a long journey, I was met by some journalists who were waiting for me in the airport, keen to announce news of my arrival.

I was booked to stay at the Grand Hotel Manila, housed in a beautiful Colonial-style building.

The country's wealthiest and most influential families lived in a residential area walled off and separated from the surrounding shantytowns. Entry was only by invitation, passing by armed guards. I was lucky enough to be invited into some of these beautiful homes.

Here, I met the most important names, all those families who were closely associated both economically and politically to the dictator's wife, Imelda Marcos. She was a big fan of Gucci bags and shoes, with many of our items in her outlandish collection.

Obviously, I also saw the city. It was rather poor, which struck me in terms of the contrast between the beautiful houses I had visited.

I was there for the opening of a space inside a massive department store that was devoted exclusively to Gucci items. The owner of the department store was named Rustan. He was very kind to me, even organising a weekend trip with his daughter and offering me a wonderful stay in a place called Boracay. We left on a Friday in a little Piper plane, crossing part of the Philippines along the south coast of Manila, where we spied crystal clear waters and white beaches. We landed on a green lawn for a landing strip. I spent a long weekend in a bungalow on the beach, which was truly beautiful and relaxing.

I also met and enjoyed some time with a handsome man who was half Spanish and half Filipino, the owner of immense sugar paper (cardstock) crops.

In Seoul, I went to the opening of the Gucci corner the city's swankiest hotel, the Shilla. An evening was organised, during which I was to give a welcome speech to everyone in English.

The Korean family that owned the Gucci corner of the hotel will forever remain in my heart. They treated me almost like a daughter. I met the entire family – the father, the mother and the two daughters, one of whom was in charge of the Gucci store. They showed me the whole city, which in my opinion was not exactly beautiful, being a mix of Eastern tradition and modernity. We often went out to dine together. They would take me to typical Korean restaurants, a kind of Chinese/Japanese cuisine, where we would eat Japanese-style seated on the floor. Before my departure, the family presented me with a splendid gift, a sapphire necklace. Their generosity and hospitality moved me to tears.

Next, I was off to Aruba in the Netherlands Antilles. After a long flight, I had to open a new Gucci store. The Italian owners had originally come to simply visit this enchanting place then decided to stay for good.

At that time, Aruba was a strategic point for shopping. Americans came in droves, since everything was tax-free. This also included the Gucci merchandise.

As soon as I arrived, I saw that my hotel was right in front of a stunning beach. I grabbed a towel and immediately set off in my swimsuit to go lay in the sun. Owing to my exhaustion from the trip, I quickly fell asleep. I woke up quite some time later and went back to my room. Looking in the mirror, I was almost purple with sunburn! My face was unpresentable. The only thing I had with me was some pressed powder, which I patted abundantly over my face. In the evening, there was the cutting of the ribbon where I was the special guest. My 'suntan' was truly embarrassing – I reckon everyone must have noticed!

Towards the end of the 1980s, in addition to dealing with the buyers and opening new Gucci outlets, I got serious about creating an historical archive dedicated to the family business. The idea was to collect precious source materials – photographs, handbag models and documents – with the aim of organising an exhibition that would travel to cities worldwide. To this end, I wrote letters to the celebrities who had patronised our stores over the years, explaining that I was putting together materials that could evoke the wonderful history of the Gucci brand.

I wrote to Gina Lollobrigida, who gladly sent me two handbags from her collection. Two more valuable samples belonging to Ava Gardner reached me through the movie star's secretary.

Recalling the aristocrats who had been Gucci clients, I contacted the Crespi family from Bologna. They sent me an enchanting 1950s toiletries kit which had belonged to their grandfather. It was full of small perfume bottles. At my father's place, I found an old leather bag dating from the 1940s decorated with a blue and yellow ribbon with his initials stamped in gold.

Gianluca Brozzetti, head of the marketing office, was instrumental in helping me in this enterprise. The recovered material remained with the Gucci business, although the archive itself came to nothing. Yet my efforts were a great help to all the new managers who in later years took over.

My father was spending more and more time in New York. I took advantage of this to visit him in that fascinating city, always coming back in the highest spirits, my arms full of parcels.

I was happy to have reached an important position in the family business through my own efforts.

It was during this period that I met Vittorio Gassman, who often was in Florence to visit his drama school. He even came to a cocktail party at my place. A dear friend of mine, who worked in the theatre with him, suggested I invite Gassman to a dinner party. I welcomed the idea enthusiastically, so my friend sent out an invitation to the great actor. Shortly before the party, the bell rang and I went anxiously to the door. I heard a voice say, "Flower delivery!" When I opened the door, I was greeted with a red extravaganza – a huge bouquet of roses with a card: "Forgive me for not coming tonight. I expect to see you at the theatre tomorrow," signed by Vittorio Gassman. After that, we met up often. One day, he called me at the office. His call went to the switchboard. The operator then stammered, "Signora Gucci... Umm... A man by the name of Vittorio Gassman would like to speak to you." "Of course," I said, "put him through." I took Gassman to a Gucci fashion show and obviously felt very glamorous by his side. I also often went to see the actor's theatre productions – how exciting it was to watch him perform on stage.

A difficult time

Then came a tough period, marked by constant quarrels and power struggles amongst the various generations of Gucci. The future of the family business, in spite of its growing success, was in jeopardy – a number of its members hoped it would go on as a family enterprise whilst others wanted a joint-stock company listed on the stock exchange. And, as is known, Tuscans are famous for their litigious character.

For my father in particular, this was a truly painful period. He was frustrated and felt like his own father and brothers did not appreciate him. He strongly wished to be acknowledged as the company's official designer – which to all effects he was – so as to go on with his projects without being continually challenged. After struggling for years, at his age he no longer wanted to be answerable to anyone. He was restless, physically exhausted and resentful. Knowing that he was brooding over something, I feared for the future.

I remember a meeting in the boardroom with all company executives, which I also attended. My father started talking about an idea of his. My grandfather grew so incensed that he actually shouted him down in front of everybody: "Paolo, shut up and listen!" My father left the room. I felt humiliated too.

At that time, I didn't see much of my father. We usually communicated by phone, as he now lived mostly in England and the U.S. In addition to his house in the Sussex town of Rusper, he also had an apartment in New York.

My father also had some challenges in his private life. He had met an English woman and kept company with her for some time. I didn't like her very much. Who knows, maybe it was the sort of intuition only a daughter can have, but in time my instinct proved correct.

She passed herself off as his wife, probably because on a journey together to Haiti they had celebrated a pretend wedding – since he was still married to my mother. (My father often went to Haiti for the excellent processed leather turned out by the local factories.)

Having "married" him for money, she did her best to falsify documents. She was a horrible woman. When their relationship was over, she would not leave him alone, demanding all of his money and staking claim to his assets as if she had been his actual wife. Yet all this was blatantly false. After years of disputes, she moved to the United States, the country of women's rights, and filed a claim against him for not paying her alimony. As a result, my father could not go to New York for some time. One day, he called her to say he wanted to put an end to their fights and made her an "offer" – "If I go there, I'll give you 4 million dollars." She agreed.

So, my father went. Right after leaving the airport, he called her to set a time and place to meet to give her the "tidy little sum". My father was unaware that she had laid a trap for him. Wanting a much bigger sum, she had reported his arrival in the country to the police. My father was met by police officers, who arrested him. He was in detention for twenty days. The experience left him truly scarred.

Exhausted by the tensions in the family, it was only his many ideas for new handbags and garments that restored his bubbling enthusiasm. Every time he was in Florence, he would meet with Roberto Meciani, his favourite designer. They had a warm relationship and understood each other right off the bat, managing to create lovely and original products together, from scarves to handbags.

Still, my father's dream was to create a brand of his own. While waiting for that to happen, he devised a logo with his initials, PG, in gold and stamped on a black horse saddle with a red border. This dream grew into a fixation for him. For the time being, however, everything was at a standstill while he waited to reach an agreement with his brothers, hoping it would happen soon. I didn't want to get involved so went on with my job. But it pained me to see him restless, like a pent up lion.

Meanwhile, my cousins – Roberto's children, Cosimo and Filippo, and Giorgio's children, Alessandro and Guccio – had also entered the family business. They sided with their parents.

The trouble the Gucci family went through from here on out, and which climaxed with the final sale of the family shares, was due precisely to the company's financial structure. The company charter stated that shares were inherited by male family members only. When the childless Uncle Vasco passed away in 1975, his shares were split evenly between his brothers Aldo and Rodolfo. Aldo gave 10% of his stock to his three sons – Giorgio, Paolo and Roberto – who thus became first-time shareholders. Rodolfo did not give any of his to his only son, Maurizio, who was still a child at that time. Maurizio, however, inherited 50% of his father's shares when the latter died in 1983. Thus, he found himself in a much stronger financial position within the company than the other family shareholders.

Meanwhile, my father's desire to create his own "Paolo Gucci" line had become increasingly pressing. He felt this was his personal payback towards his family, after so many years of malice and chagrin. Yet, he himself was a changed man, surrounded by people who pushed him to harbour negative feelings against his own kin. His brothers and father left him to his own devices during that difficult period. Only my mother tried to soothe him, urging him to stay calm and to avoid any friction with the others.

I was worried sick that my father would sell his shares and leave the family business. I knew how impulsive he could be and that once an idea got into his head, it would be impossible to make him change his mind. The more the others tried to thwart him, the more headstrong he became.

Finally, Paolo tried to reach an agreement with his father and brothers on starting a new company – the Gucci Licensing Service – to manage Gucci brand designs and projects, with him as acting president. Their acceptance would have led to a separate and independent management of the two companies, to the advantage of everyone. But the others did not like his idea – they thought it was too competitive and did not want Paolo to be independent.

Personally, I think they made a mistake. Not only would this solution have made my father happy but if the Gucci brand had have been managed separately, it would have lasted much longer.

After Rodolfo's death in 1983, the shares inherited by Maurizio were frozen for tax reasons.

Whilst Maurizio waited to resume his full-time role in the family business, Maria Martellini, a professor at Milan's Bocconi University, assumed guardianship of his shares and became president of Società Guccio Gucci Italia. That was when my father thought about throwing his weight behind Maurizio, giving him a part of his shares, in order to create a shareholding structure that would be favourable to both. The project never took off. To this day, I don't know whether this was owing to Maurizio or to my father. Perhaps Maurizio was the one who backed out of the deal.

I experienced all this from a distance. I saw my uncles rarely and when I did, we chose not to discuss such matters. Yet a thorn had lodged in my heart. I could hardly imagine a way out, knowing all too well how petulant they all were.

Refusing to get emotionally involved (especially with my father), I kept telling myself that these were not my problems. I was young and determined to build a future of my own.

And so, I just kept working hard, paying no heed to the clamour around me. Lots of pressure came from my father. He kept urging me to resign from the family business. Our telephone conversations were always stressful.

Thanks to my determination, courage and insight, I did not – unlike my cousins – give in to my father's direction and demands. I was a Gucci and felt like one, but I was not a captain about to abandon ship. That was not my role. I was rather more like a member of the crew that keeps the family business on course.

At that time, Maurizio was running the show and I was able to work with him with a degree of calm.

My psychological situation was sorely tested since I was being pressured on all sides to go one way or another. If I stayed on at Gucci, I would incur my father's fury whilst leaving meant abandoning the career I had pursued in the family business.

It goes without saying that my uncles and grandfather constantly reminded me of my father's responsibility in all of this, accusing him of having made the wrong decisions. It was not an easy time for me. Having to decide on the right course without disappointing any of the parties involved meant lots of sleepless nights.

Every morning, I went to the office with a sick feeling in the pit of my stomach: "What's going to happen today?"

In 1987, the Bahrain-based Investcorp made an attractive offer to buy a stake in the Gucci company. My father looked favourably on the proposal and sold his shares to Investcorp. A little later, Aldo and his two other sons – now in the minority – followed suit. Investcorp thus acquired 50% of the corporate shares, with the other half remaining with Maurizio Gucci.

The sale of the shares turned out to be a disaster and all the more so for us children. How could this have happened? Nobody had given a thought to us – we, who had grown up inside the family company and were so intimately connected to it. What future awaited us now?

The endless clashes and constant competition between individuals with strong temperaments who were fundamentally incapable of compromise meant the whole lot of them had lost sight of the most precious asset: our family business.

In all likelihood, the absence of a mediator also proved crucial. Guccio Gucci, the founder of the dynasty, had filled that role in the past. Driven by his enthusiasm and the wish to keep his business alive, he probably would have found the way of reaching some agreement. Yet, things took a different turn.

My own future was in jeopardy. I cried a lot. Then, thinking of my work and the good relationship I had always enjoyed with Maurizio, I went to him to set out my concerns. Maurizio reassured me: "Never mind your father. Stay here and work with me." This made me very happy. My other cousins, however, followed in their parents' footsteps and left the company.

A few years after the sale of the Gucci shares, my father won a lawsuit against Gucci America, which had tried to prevent him from producing a line of products under his own name. With this victory, he could at last officially use his name for the brand: Paolo, designed by Paolo Gucci.

After settling the issues linked to the shares he had inherited, Maurizio returned to the company and became its president. He had a very modern vision of business management and wanted to turn Gucci into a publicly-traded company. Maurizio brought with him many (perhaps too many) new, know-it-all foot soldiers. They received magnificent salaries and great benefits – personal drivers, luxury apartments in Florence, first-class travel, new desks and plush chairs (all Gucci leather, of course).

At the time, this gave us all a big jolt. The new arrivals wanted to change the marketing strategies, the work plans and everything else besides. They relocated or replaced old employees who had been with the company for thirty years. I, too, had trouble dealing with them. My role in the company was not well accepted, perhaps because I was a woman. Maurizio chose people with big names to be his collaborators. For instance, he hired Dawn Mello, who had worked for many years in the Bergdorf & Dorfman department stores in New York. Dawn Mello became the artistic director of Gucci Italia. Soon after, Dawn even introduced Maurizio to her great friend and stylist, Tom Ford.

The new managers were busy rummaging through the drawers and bookshelves for the old designs belonging to the Gucci tradition. This brings me to recount something I witnessed directly. While I was setting up an archive of the family business, I came across a sketchbook with drawings of handbags done by one Guido D'Acquino, an old worker hired by my father. Dawn Mello came to me and said, "I'll take this. I need it." I protested that it belonged to the family archive and had to stay where it was. But it didn't matter. The following day, the sketchbook was gone. I was furious and called Maurizio to tell him about it. He answered, "I know. She called me yesterday and I told her to take it."

Yes, the company had been partly sold but the Gucci name and style remained the same. Great skills were not required to put the old designs back on the market. It was a matter of making minor changes and freshening them up. The new stylists were placed on a pedestal and wildly overpaid but their job was – and still is – to merely revamp the heritage that the Guccis most brilliantly and unitedly put together over the years. The originality and creativity that appears in every Gucci-marked object belongs and will always belong to the family. Even Santo Versace confirmed as much when I recently met him at an event: "Gucci would not exist today if all of you had not been there before."

In 1991, Grandfather Aldo passed away. It was a painful event for all of us. He died in Rome, surrounded by his children and grandchildren. My father was there, too, with tears welling in his eyes. Grandfather gave him a Cartier watch that he had always worn on his wrist, perhaps as a last sign of forgiveness.

With its 50% stake in the Gucci company, Investcorp was now making trouble for Maurizio. The new shareholders wanted to get rid of the entire Gucci family. Maurizio asked Domenico del Sole for help. This well-known Italian-American lawyer had, in the earlier years, handled Rodolfo's legal issues. After many years in the company, he was appointed president of Gucci America. Domenico was considered a family friend, was trusted by all and knew the company and its secrets inside out. In my view, he proved to be a most unpleasant individual and unscrupulous profiteer. In 1993, during the last board meeting in New York, he even turned his back on Maurizio when he had asked Domenico for his support. Instead, he voted for Investcorp. Maurizio was forced to sell his stake to Investcorp, which thus became sole owner of the company.

All the Guccis were now out of the company. Financially, it was a brilliant move.

Tom Ford, who had joined in 1990 as head of the women's ready-to-wear clothing department, was interviewed by Style Magazine in December 2006. He stated that when the Gucci family departed, there wasn't even a photocopier left and said that the premises smelled mouldy. I was present at the time – the photocopiers worked just fine and there was no smell of mould.

While I was clearing my things off my desk and putting them into a box, I happened to cross paths with Tom Ford. This was a good moment for him. He was in the right place at the right time and managed to combine his personal glamour with the enormous heritage that had dropped into his lap.

Yes, we did sell the family company – the famous chicken that lays golden eggs. Even Jacqueline Kennedy sent us a telegram saying simply, "Why?"

Yet the point is that the style, the logo, the designs, the red-and-green ribbon, the bamboo handle and the hundreds of models and objects were created only by my family. We are the ones who invented a uniquely Italian style and exported it to the rest of the world. Those same objects, refashioned, can be seen in the shop windows today.

I am terribly disappointed that the newcomers to the company – the yuppie stylists and famous managers – were able to find fortune and success without being able to acknowledge this undeniable legacy and their moral indebtedness to us.

I still remember the day when I found a letter on my desk from the marketing office, for which I worked: a meeting on "Sales Strategies" had been scheduled for the following day at 10:30 a.m. at the Via delle Caldaie headquarters. The new management – from the Head of Marketing down to his assistants, plus the Human Resources and Sales Research Managers (in my view, all rather useless positions) would be there.

The following day, I went to the meeting room full of curiosity. I looked around me. There were about ten people. I was the only woman. Everyone turned to greet me in a seemingly huffy tone: "Buongiorno, Signora Gucci."

I sat down. On the table in front of my seat, I found a folder with my name on it and some papers inside. There was a similar folder for the others, too. I opened mine.

It was a handout with marketing graphs, percentages, coloured plans for sales targets, market strategies and programmes to promote the company's growth. The Head of Marketing spoke first, explaining what I had already found in my folder. His talk boiled down to a rehash of the same topics. It would have been easier for us just to read the papers in the folders. Half an hour later, the discussion took on an angry and crass turn for which there was absolutely no justification.

I was given the floor and started to explain my opinions. Once I had finished speaking, they embarrassed me with snide comments laced with coarse language. Rather than addressing any of my points, they merely wanted to deride me in front of the all-male audience. One phrase confirmed everything: "Please forgive me for this language, Signora Gucci."

Remembering Maurizio

A s I write this book, I can't avoid speaking about the tragic events in the life of Maurizio Gucci, to whose memory I wish to dedicate a loving tribute. I am looking at a marvellous black and white photo of him, yet when he comes to mind, it is with some unpleasantness. When a person we love passes away, we often remember their energy but can't reassemble their facial features, so we rely on pictures to help.

It was November 1971. That afternoon, nearly the whole Gucci family had gathered in front of the Odeon cinema in downtown Florence. Maurizio was there, along with his father Rodolfo, my parents, my sister Elizabeth and I, almost all of my cousins, many company employees.

I was fifteen and had taken great pains to look my best for the occasion. My hair was curly at the time and I had done everything possible to straighten it. Around my neck was a nice foulard – a Gucci one, of course – in case of rain. Maurizio was then 23. He was wearing a light suit with bell-bottom trousers (which were all the rage!), a dark shirt and a light-coloured tie.

Uncle Rodolfo, whose nickname was Foffo, was always very generous and loving with his nieces and nephews. Every Christmas, he would send us a large beige and blue box from Cova, the famous Milan pâtisserie. Inside, we would find an enormous panettone and all kinds of sweets and pastries – torrone, chocolates, marron glacé, and much more besides.

For us, it was a real treat.

That evening, Uncle Rodolfo had booked the entire hall of the Odeon cinema to show his film, *Il cinema nella mia vita*. Even after he had quit acting, he remained a great lover of movies.

In fact, Rodolfo often behaved somewhat theatrically. I remember one day in the office at the Scandicci production factory, he started to harangue the staff. "Good morning, Signori, Signore and Signorine, how are you? Everything fine?" Then, he slowly turned around and started talking to the shelves on the wall. A female employee took him gently by the arm and led him back to the middle of the room, where he continued talking, oblivious to everything!

Uncle Rodolfo had a collection of several hundred films which he would always watch with great enthusiasm. There were all kinds of pictures, from Charlie Chaplin to Fellini, as well as those in which he had acted before the war. A true film library.

Il cinema nella mia vita consisted of different episodes that he himself had filmed of his family life, his accomplishments, the actress Sandra Ravel, and Maurizio when he was a child. The enchanting scene in which Sandra is running happily and without a care next to little Maurizio particularly struck me. She had died young and it was truly moving to see her like that. When we filed out of the cinema hall, I went up to Maurizio and gave him a big hug. I loved him a lot and he was quite moved. I gave Uncle Rodolfo a hug too and congratulated him on his picture.

Many years passed before I saw Maurizio again. He now lived in Milan, where he led a peaceful existence in the loving embrace of his father and Aunt Tallia, the woman who brought him up after his mother died.

Maurizio completed his higher education and earned a Law Degree. Then, he went on to work in the Milan Gucci store, before finally moving to New York where he became Grandfather Aldo's assistant.

Rodolfo absolutely doted on Maurizio, never remarrying so that he could devote himself entirely to his son. Rodolfo doted on his son in every way, ending up being too protective and in some ways overwhelming. Still, at seventeen, Maurizio had met Patrizia Reggiani, who became his first girlfriend.

He immediately fell in love with her. Uncle Rodolfo never thought much of Patrizia. He was a little jealous of her and thought his son was too young to get engaged. Calling her "the truck driver's daughter", he became dead set against their marriage. But their relationship endured and in 1972, Maurizio and Patrizia did marry – against Rodolfo's will.

As often happens, the father's opposition only strengthened their resolve. Nobody in the family attended the wedding, not even Uncle Rodolfo. After getting married, Maurizio and Patrizia went to live in New York for some time before eventually returning to Italy.

I will never forget that March morning in 1995. I was at home in Florence, busy as usual.

Around 11:30, the telephone rang. It was Maria Gentile, a dear friend who had worked with my father for many years. In an alarmed tone, Maria said: "Turn on the TV!" I asked her why, since I never watched TV in the morning. I went to turn on the television with Maria still on the line. "They shot Maurizio!" she said. I asked her to repeat the sentence. "What, they shot Maurizio? There must be some mistake!" Meanwhile, the TV showed harrowing images of Maurizio on a stretcher, Maurizio's daughters in tears and Paola Franchi (his last partner) absolutely devastated.

Maurizio was killed on Via Palestro in front of his office. Three shots of a pistol were fired, with the lethal one striking him in the head. Almost mute and very frightened, I immediately called my father in England where news surely had not yet arrived.

"Hello, Father, I have some very, very bad news!"

"What is it?"

"Maurizio has been killed; he was shot!"

Words failed him for a moment, then he said: "God knows what trouble he had gotten himself into!"

I put down the receiver and burst into tears.

He was so young, barely 47. I loved him a lot and we had worked together in the family business for many years. He used to come to the Gucci factory in Florence with that self-assured Milanese air, always followed by a group of aides, which he replaced quite often. The only one who stayed on with him was his faithful driver, Luigi Pirovano.

Certainly, Maurizio's lifestyle was very different from that of the other Guccis. Life had given him everything he could ever want, his every whim could be indulged. My grandfather Aldo in New York used to take the subway to work but Maurizio would never have done such a thing.

Since his father's death, he had changed a lot. He wanted to have a hand in everything when it came to the family business. He felt cramped in Florence and talked about moving the headquarters to Milan. He found the family stewardship of our company somewhat obsolete and wanted to see Gucci listed on the stock exchange and producing items that were more commercial and would sell more easily.

Still, in my opinion, the real Maurizio was a good man, albeit a fragile and insecure one.

Unfortunately, he unknowingly surrounded himself with people who took advantage of him. At heart, though, my cousin loved life and the simple things.

I remember how passionate he was about the sea and sailing. One evening in Portofino, he invited me to a party for the launch of the Gucci-sponsored Italia. At the restaurant that evening, I saw how happy he was amid the schooner's crew, overjoyed that he could share his love for the sea with them.

During the time we worked together, he would encourage me, tell me I was clever and had character. He inspired me to keep going in spite of any setbacks.

Maurizio's death led to a free-for-all in farfetched news. The newspapers published all kinds of falsehoods, alleging he had engaged in shady business. Everybody had a different opinion.

It was a terrible scandal, which someone called a "tasty media banquet". I tried to step in. I gave interviews to supply the actual facts – but it was in vain. The scandal unleashed by Maurizio Gucci's murder unexpectedly overwhelmed us, embroiling all of us personally and severely.

In the days following the murder, all Italian and international newspapers rushed to publish their stories. They wrote streams of words and articles about our family, describing us even in the absence of first-hand knowledge. We found ourselves splashed onto the front pages, where everybody was reading about how the Guccis were some sort of dynasty made up of quarrelsome people ready to wage war against each other.

Revoltingly described and slandered by the media, it almost seemed as if we were being blamed for what had happened. I received dozens of telephone calls from journalists who wanted to know the behind-the-scene details of our family and glean more information relating to the murder.

Many people external to our family gave entirely dishonest interviews on the matter for the sole purpose of putting themselves in the spotlight. At first, these articles also contained accusations of shady dealings that seemed to implicate Maurizio himself.

For almost two years, the slanderous words and reports even confounded the police investigation into the events, since even the investigators themselves didn't know what to make of it all. Only after two years did police arrest Reggiani on the charge of being behind Maurizio's murder.

English and American TV knocked at my door, assuring me they would be careful and discreet about any information I gave them, but they proceeded to act in bad faith. In the U.S., we were described as a family that produced handbags made from the skin of pig's ears. My grandfather Aldo was portrayed as a sort of mafia character. The picture that emerged was mucky and most distressing.

In my interviews on the Maurizio Costanzo Show, La vita in diretta, Rai3, and other TV channels, I aimed to set the story straight with the actual facts. I passionately defended my family from the slander and rumours that had filled the news.

Indeed, I suffered and continue to suffer great personal damage from Maurizio's murder. Patrizia Reggiani, Maurizio's ex-wife and the person who ordered the crime, went by the same name as me. For years, she introduced herself as Patrizia Gucci, causing much confusion and damaging me and my private and professional image.

I must add that many newspapers, in an effort to attract attention and sell more copies, have repeatedly written articles referring to this woman by my name. This was and still is an offense punishable by Italian law, given that Reggiani divorced Maurizio in 1994. Thus, she lost any right to use the surname Gucci, which no longer belongs to her (because in Italy, women are no longer allowed to use their husband's surname after divorce).

There was a big crowd at Maurizio's funeral – there were lots of photographers and relatives, including my mother who had known Maurizio since he was a boy and was very fond of him. Of course, there were his two daughters Alessandra and Allegra, and his ex-wife Patrizia Reggiani (hiding behind a black veil). It wasn't until two years later, in 1997, that she was arrested and charged with having arranged the murder. An unexpected heartbreak.

Maurizio was the last descendant of the Gucci dynasty to run the family business. Today, the Gucci brand name continues to be very popular but the soul has been tugged out of it.

The past as a backdrop to the present

Sometimes it is difficult to understand whether a chain of events that shapes our lives, and which we call destiny, is like a magnet pulling us in directions we perhaps don't wish to take, or whether the path is set. In the tangle of emotions that certain events throw up, it is nonetheless important to seek answers and take the opportunity to reflect deeply. Valuing our experiences, even tragic ones, makes us stronger and more able to face down troubles.

That is how things went for me.

1995 was the worst year I have ever experienced. Maurizio died in March. In August, he was followed by my Nanna Olwen and, in October, by my father.

The ensuing sale of the family business was certainly not my decision but one made by my elders. I never imagined that the future would change so drastically, that I would so suddenly lose the role I had in the family undertaking bearing my name. I went from being a career woman, a future shareholder, to a Gucci without the shelter of the family company – a company, moreover, that carried such an important and at times overwhelming surname.

The sacrifices and hardships that date back to the years when I was working seemed to have vanished. And yet out of that indelible Gucci past, I have emerged with greater self-confidence and greater self-assurance, as a woman who has rebuilt her life from scratch. If I go over my past in all its richness and intensity,

I find that every detail of what I saw and experienced is precious to me. It seems almost as if I have gone to a faculty of studies that teaches a decidedly original subject – a true university of life that has taken me from marketing strategies to a treasure trove of human relationships, both the good and the bad. Successfully working through the complicated relationships I had with both my father and my family as a whole has allowed me to understand other people in all their intricacies, for better or for worse.

I can say that I inherited a sensitivity to all things beautiful and elegant from my father. Indeed, he could turn a mere design that he had casually sketched with the moistened tip of a pencil, into a work art. The secret of the success of the Gucci style and of that empire of good taste, hinged exactly on this, and on dedication and steadfastness. Day after day, from daybreak to nightfall, was spent in the shop and in the production factory. All the Guccis throughout the generations were endlessly devoted to their work, always seeking the new and never neglecting the importance of dedicating time to their staff in the workplace. The Gucci status symbol became a reality long ago.

When I left the family company, I felt completely lost. This forced me, in spite of myself, to find a way to go on.

I no longer had to get up early in the morning to go to work, nor did I have to carefully consider how to dress that day for the necessary elegant and impeccable Gucci store look, nor did I need to rush to the office to be there on time. Now, I could wake up whenever I wished, put on a pair of sneakers and go shopping at the market. After such a long time, I was tasting a strange freedom I had never known before. Having grown up being accustomed to working, I was restless and struggled to discover how to pursue my own interests. I reflected on things for a long time but it wasn't easy to get used to the idea of having new bosses at some new job, who would challenge my suggestions or give me tasks that were not in line with my expectations. I had spent too much time trying to distinguish myself and to achieve an important position. Job offers did come my way but many of them were only because of my name and not because of my qualities. So, they were not enticing. The family imprint, based on a work ethic and above all on that magical teaching, was crucial to every decision I made. In the past. I had always achieved everything through my own dogged efforts and determination, and wished for my perseverance, loyalty, resoluteness and love to show through even in my smallest deeds.

When my father died, another cornerstone vanished. It was a difficult time. I found solace in reading books, even on Eastern philosophy, and later took up meditation and yoga courses. These helped me enormously to rebuild my life in a positive way and to concentrate on future resolutions.

It was a great joy to start painting again. The right opportunity came through a member of Investcorp, who I had met through the family business. Mr Abdul Jaleel Al Ansari organised an exhibition for me at Manama, the capital of Bahrain in the Persian Gulf. I started working with the utmost resolution. I had to make an agreement with the customers on the subject of my paintings, which had to be approved by a government commission since Arab countries do not allow the portrayal of violent subjects or nudity, nor anything else that might be deemed offensive to their religion. At that time, I mostly worked on figurative painting in oils or acrylic paints. My themes were landscapes, flowers and birds. It took almost a year to organise the exhibition but fortunately, people liked my paintings.

For the venue, I was asked to choose between the Manama Art Centre and the Hotel Le Méridien. I chose the latter, thinking that my paintings would have a larger public there. One corner of the main reception hall was made available for my collection. I flew there on my own and stayed at Le Méridien for twenty days. It was an enchanting hotel, full of marble halls and crystal objects, all very high class, overlooking a stretch of golden beach.

One day when I was sitting in the hall in front of my paintings, I was told that Sheikh Khalifa bin Salman Al Khalifa, Bahrain's

Prime Minister, had come to the hotel for a political meeting. The Prime Minister happened to walk through the reception hall and was struck by my paintings. I still remember how it happened: he stopped in front of them, surrounded by his bodyguards, who asked the other visitors to move away. I was almost frightened. The Prime Minister, wearing his white head covering with the black cord and a long brown ceremonial cloak, stopped in front of my favourite painting: a hoopoe in flight. Silently and quite attentively, he studied all my paintings. Then finally, his secretary raised his hand with all fingers outspread, signifying that he would buy five. I was absolutely delighted. The secretary said he would get back to me. After a few days' wait, during which time I was full of anxiety and hope, he called to confirm the purchase. I commended myself for my daring and nerve, thoroughly savouring this unexpected personal success.

The state of Bahrain (whose name means "between two seas") stayed in my heart to such an extent that the following year, I went back for a vacation. I visited Oman as well. Thanks to my friendship with the French ambassador, Georges Duquin, I also met the Prime Minister's brother, the Emir Isa bin Salman Al Khalifa. I met him in his private garden by the sea where he went for tea on Fridays. When we were introduced, he said, "So you are the famous Italian painter!" And then he bought one of my paintings as well.

In those years, painting became my profession. I had other exhibitions in Florence and abroad. My painting grew more mature, as I now was doing both figurative and abstract. I still paint today, a practise that has always fascinated me.

Having the need to think things over and understand the world around me, I next decided to write a book: *Il piccolo libro della semplicità*. It was published and enjoyed great success, staying on the bestseller list for two weeks and selling 70,000 copies.

Following this, some interesting proposals came my way. The chief editor of the well-known women's weekly magazine "Donna

Moderna" asked me to write an advice column on household matters: how to organise a wardrobe, prepare for a dinner party, tidy up your desk, wear only five pairs of shoes, what fragrances to use for the bedroom, and so on.

I was beginning to find my way and was getting my life back together. Once again, my family name was a source of pride for me, no longer just a burden. Even now, when I'm at the airport going somewhere, I hear: "You have a nice name!" Indeed, my name is more famous than a Beatles song. And yet, there was a time when it was only a problem for me. True freedom really does come only from within.

Sometime later, I decided to write another book, *Single, il fascino della donna libera.* I wanted to narrate the experience of a woman who had achieved a lot without betting everything on married life. There is no need to feel lonely and unhappy just because you don't have a man by your side. Indeed, it is better to use those moments of solitude to rediscover yourself and your feminine qualities. We can derive benefit from any kind of experience – even the seemingly negative ones can ultimately reveal the positive.

This book, too, was a success and ended up being translated into eight languages. I had gone to the heart of a profound issue. A few years later, I wrote *Charme, l'arte della seduzione.* It was a light, fun book, describing how a woman can charm men with her natural gifts and the self-assurance that comes from within. Seduction is an art and it needs to be fine-tuned over time as we grow increasingly aware of our true allure.

I was lucky to have brushes with the business world many more times, from Japan to the U.S.A. That's when I too became a stylist. Since I can no longer use my family name, I devised my own brand name: Patti Patti, the nickname I had as a child. I, too, started designing handbags. Simple handbags, starting from a colour – a practical, pleasant, modern way of looking at this accessory.

To sum up

L ate August, 2011.
Going through the newspapers, I was drawn to a bold headline, *Inauguration of the Gucci Museum in Florence – 90 Years of History Since the Establishment of the Gucci Trademark.*
The article reported a world-class event to be held in the presence of Florence Mayor Matteo Renzi, American celebrities, and important people in the world of fashion. I waited for an invitation, which never came. So, after a few days I took pen and paper – with my Gucci letterhead, of course – and wrote to M. Henri F. Pinault, CEO of the PPR Group. I was worried that for the umpteenth time, they would tell the story of my family incorrectly and unfairly. In the past, PPR Group had prompted biased articles in the press. And, in any case, I had not received any invitation.

In that letter, I wrote about how keen I was to have my family portrayed with the importance and recognition it deserved, and that the present management of our one-time company should underscore its admiration for and gratitude towards us. Finally, I wrote that I would not stand for any dubious adjectives or improprieties. About a week later, I received a reply.

The letter had been sent from Casellina, not Paris. I opened the envelope with much curiosity. The reply came not from my addressee but from Patrizio di Marco, CEO of the Italian Group.

He wrote to reassure me that nothing offensive or untrue would be said. Inside the envelope was also an invitation to the event – not for the day of the inauguration day but for the following day.

I learned that they had decided to have two soirees: the first a gala evening with red carpet, the second for staff.

Saddened, I went into my walk-in wardrobe and with some irritation, started pulling out all the Gucci fashion products I own: 80 handbags, 30 foulards, about 40 belts, 15 evening pochettes or so, boots, short leather skirts and a long cognac-coloured deerskin skirt. Full-length jackets, some wristwatches, bracelets and a red jacket with tiger head buttons from when I was sixteen. In short, in my life there is a part of the company's history and its products that nobody can take away from me.

I am proud to be a Gucci, proud of its legacy – of its intensely-coloured humanity, character, style and creativity. And I want the memory of that great story to endure.

Thanks to

Maria Rosa Brachetti
Paola Masi
Enzo Biliotti
Concettina Cipolla
Dante Ferrari
Maria Gentile
Josef Cantatore
Giuliana Tozzi
Luigi Limberti
Paolo Biagion

Made in the USA
Middletown, DE
23 February 2022

61731289R00097